The Man Who Knew God

The Man Who Knew God

Decoding Jeremiah

Mordecai Schreiber

LEXINGTON BOOKS
A division of
ROWMAN & LITTLEFIELD PUBLISHERS, INC.
Lanham • Boulder • New York • Toronto • Plymouth, UK

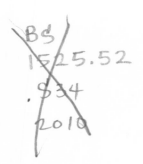
Published by Lexington Books
A division of Rowman & Littlefield Publishers, Inc.
A wholly owned subsidiary of The Rowman & Littlefield Publishing Group, Inc.
4501 Forbes Boulevard, Suite 200, Lanham, Maryland 20706
http://www.lexingtonbooks.com

Estover Road, Plymouth PL6 7PY, United Kingdom

British Library Cataloguing in Publication Information Available

Library of Congress Cataloging-in-Publication Data

Schreiber, Mordecai.
  The man who knew God : decoding Jeremiah / Mordecai Schreiber.—1st. ed.
    p. cm.
  Includes bibliographical references and index.
  ISBN 978-0-7391-4345-2 (cloth : alk. paper)
  ISBN 978-0-7391-4346-9 (pbk. : alk. paper)
  ISBN 978-0-7391-4347-6 (electronic)
  1. Bible. O.T. Jeremiah—Criticism, interpretation, etc. I. Title.
  BS1525.52.S34 2010
  224'.206—dc22   2009036731

The paper used in this publication meets the minimum requirements of American
National Standard for Information Sciences—Permanence of Paper for Printed Library
Materials, ANSI/NISO Z39.48-1992.

Printed in the United States of America

Contents

Preface

He has had an enormous impact on my life. I got to know him when I was very young, and as I grew older his impact on me kept growing. Now, in my mature years, I look to him once again for answers to the great questions of life. In particular, I would like to better understand God through him. The more I read and reread and study his words, the more convinced I become he knew God more personally and more intimately than perhaps even Moses. This knowledge enabled him to understand the human condition and human history better than anyone else before or after. He is as relevant today as he was 2,600 years ago. He is certainly worth listening to.

I am speaking of the biblical prophet Jeremiah.

For as long as I can remember, he has spoken to me. I remember it well. It was 1947. I was eight years old. I lived in a town called Haifa, on the edge of what many call the Holy Land. On November 29 of that year something happened that changed history forever. The world voted to divide my native land into two states—a Jewish state and an Arab state. For us Jews it was history's eleventh hour. In Europe, where most of us lived, we were rounded up in nearly every country of this most civilized of continents and sent to die in gas chambers and burn in crematoria. Some of those who espoused the faith of the gentle man from Galilee chose to play God and perpetrated upon us their own nefarious vision of Dante's inferno. The skeletal remnants of that greatest crime in all of human history were now herded into displaced people's camps and had nowhere to go. The dream of the return to Zion, first dreamed 2,600 years ago during Jeremiah's lifetime, could no longer be deferred. Jews the world over knew it was time to go home.

Boatloads of Holocaust survivors arrived in Haifa harbor. Jews from Arab countries and from the remote corners of Asia also arrived in great numbers. And as they kept coming, he seemed to be walking among us, reconnecting us to our long history in this biblical land. And I remember how his words were on everyone's lips:

> A voice is heard in Ramah,
> Wailing, bitter cry,

Rachel is mourning her children
Refusing to be consoled
For her children,
Now gone.

And God said:
Do not cry.
Do not shed tears.
For your labor will be rewarded.
For they will return from the enemy's land.
There is hope in your future,
Your children shall return to their border. (31:14-16)

And somehow I felt then and there he was talking to me, and that he knew me, and I knew him.

Note on the Translation of the Bible

There are numerous English translations of the Hebrew Bible. Most have been done by Christians, who refer to this book as the Old Testament, and some by Jews, who call it *tanakh* (acronym for Torah, Prophets and Writings). No two translations are identical. In fact, they all vary greatly. There are several reasons for this. First, the Bible is an ancient text, written in a certain social and ideological context many centuries ago. Second, the Hebrew text was written over a period of centuries, and the language of David is not the language of Jeremiah. Third, a good number of the words appear only once or twice and the meaning is no longer clear. Fourth, the language is often metaphoric or hyperbolic and the meaning has to be guessed at. Fifth, many of the words cannot be translated directly into English, and require an explanation. Sixth, most translations of the Bible are done by believers who have a partisan point of view and tend to tilt the translation in their direction in such ways that can alter the original meaning to support the translator's beliefs.

A good example of a partisan translation is the way the last word of the 23rd Psalm has been rendered since the time of the King James Version four hundred years ago. The translation reads: "And I shall dwell in the house of the Lord *forever*." The word "forever" implies that life continues after death, hence this Psalm has been the most common text recited at both Jewish and Christian funerals. In reality, the original Hebrew word is *l'orech yamim*, which means "for many years." It is only in recent years that this has been corrected in such Jewish Bibles as the new JPS version, and in Christian equivalents such as The Jerusalem Bible.

Bible translation is an unending "work in progress," with new translations appearing every few years, as each new translator attempts to improve on his or her predecessors. I still like the King James Version the best, but it has its limitations, not the least of which is that it is written in the kind of English we no longer speak. Consequently, the biblical texts in this book do not reflect any particular translation, but rather my best attempt to come as close to the original text as possible.

One last comment: One of the most irksome Bible translation problems is how to translate the Hebrew name of God, consisting of the four Hebrew letters Yod Heh Vav Heh, or YHVH. In Jewish tradition, this word is unpronounceable, since no one other than the High Priest of old knew how to pronounce it. Historically, due to Saint Jerome who provided the first translation of the Bible into Latin (the Vulgate), it became Jehovah, which is a combination of the four letters YHVH with the vowels of the Hebrew word *adonai*, or Master, which is the way Jews have always said this word. Historically, English translations of the Bible, both Gentile and Jewish, have rendered it as "Lord," another way of saying master. Biblical scholars in recent times have opted for a variety of renditions such as Yahweh, Yahwe, Yahveh, or Yahve, which presume to approximate the way it was originally pronounced. Some, seeking accuracy, simply leave it as YHWH, or, in some cases, YHVH. I did not find any of these attempts satisfactory, and it seems to me that the word "Lord," while still used in the United Kingdom, is largely passé in today's world, while "Master" by itself (rather than, for example, Master of the Universe) does not convey the desired meaning. Therefore, I chose to translate YHVH as Adonai.

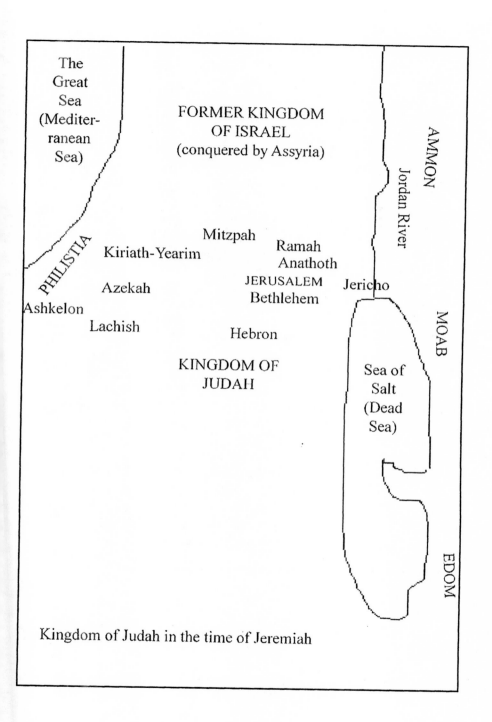

Kingdom of Judah in the time of Jeremiah

Timeline of Events in the Book of Jeremiah

(Years are BCE [before the common era])

639 - Josiah is crowned king at age eight.

626 - Jeremiah becomes prophet.

621 - Book of the Law is found. Josiah launches a religious reform.

612 - Nineveh is destroyed by Babylon. Assyrian empire loses its preeminence.

608 - Josiah dies at Megiddo. Jehoahaz, his heir, is deposed by Egypt. His brother, Jehoiakim, replaces him.

605 - Babylon's Nebuchadnezzar defeats Egypt and Assyria at Charchemish, putting an end to the empire of Assyria.

601 - Jehoiakim makes alliance with Egypt.

597 - Nebuchadnezzar takes Jerusalem after the death of Jehoiakim and the crowning of his son, Jehoiachin, who is exiled to Babylon. Zedekiah, Jeoiachin's uncle, becomes king of Judah.

593 - Nebuchadnezzar is busy putting down an uprising in Babylon.

592 - Zedekiah seizes the opportunity and makes an alliance with his small neighboring nations and with Egypt against Babylon.

588 - Babylon begins the siege of Jerusalem.

586 - Egypt attempts to come to Judah's help but fails. Jerusalem is taken and destroyed. Zedekiah and the royal family are executed. The Babylonian Exile begins.

585 - Gedaliah is made governor of Judah. He is assassinated. Jeremiah is carried off to Egypt with Judean exiles.

Chronology of the Book of Jeremiah

The book of Jeremiah does not follow a chronological order. The book consists of prophecies, mostly written in a poetic form, and prose narratives of events occurring during Jeremiah's lifetime. Its 52 chapters contain sections and verses within chapters which belong elsewhere. It is not possible to establish a complete chronological order for every chapter and verse, but a general reconstruction is possible. Jeremiah lives during the time of the following kings of Judah (years are BCE and refer to years of rule; there is often a margin of error of one year):

Josiah son of Amon (639-608), 31 years
Jehoahaz (or Shallum) son of Josiah (608), three months
Jehoiakim (originally Eliakim) son of Josiah (608-597), 11 years
Jehoiachin (or Coniah, or Jeconiah) son of Jehoiakim (597), three months
Zedekiah (originally Mattaniah) son of Josiah (597-586), 11 years

Chapter 1
Jeremiah is called to be a prophet at about age 12, in 626 BCE. The text is silent on his formative years.
Chapter 2
Jeremiah begins to prophesy c. 618, at the close of Josiah's reform. He accuses his people of betraying the covenant.
Chapter 3
Verses 1-15 continue with his previous exhortations. Verses 16-18 refer to the disappearance of the Holy Ark, and to Jeremiah's vision of the return from exile and the return to God. They belong to the time of the destruction of Jerusalem in 586.
Chapters 4-9
The focus of these chapters is the "enemy from the north." We are still in the reign of Josiah. Nebuchadnezzar, the enemy from the north, is yet to appear. Jeremiah begins his 40-year-long campaign to make his people aware of the existential danger from the north. His words fall on deaf ears.
Chapter 10
Verse 11 is the only verse in the book written in Aramaic. It belongs around 597 or later, after the Jehoiachin exile. Jeremiah is addressing the exiles in Babylon in the vernacular of their new home. Verse 25 (included in the Pass-

over Haggadah) belongs around 586 at the time of the fall of Jerusalem.

Chapter 11

This chapter takes us back to the time following the Josianic reform, as Jeremiah tries to reiterate the laws of the book of Deuteronomy and the dire consequences of failing to obey them. Here we also learn about the plot against Jeremiah by his own hometown priests, which probably happens later on.

Chapter 12

This chapter is too hard to date. It could belong after the fall, or it could be a vision of the fall dating to the time of Josiah or Jehoiachin.

Chapter 13

Here we go "back to the future," to around 597, the time of Jehoiachin's exile. The beginning verses may date back to the prophet's early period during the reign of Josiah.

Chapters 14-19

Here we have a series of prophecies which defy a clear timeframe. They are vintage Jeremiah, and could have been repeated by him on various occasions between the time of Josiah and the time of Zedekiah and the fall of Jerusalem, a period of some 40 years.

Chapter 20

Here we have the first of several stories about the attempts of the ruling class (priests and court officials) to stop Jeremiah from prophesying through physical punishment and imprisonment. This is typical of the time of the siege of Jerusalem in the days of Zedekiah (597-586).

Chapter 21

It is the time of the siege (around 587), and the king sends emissaries to ask Jeremiah to pray to God and perform a miracle to save Judah. Jeremiah knows it is too late for miracles.

Chapter 22

Here we have a reference to Shallum, the other name of King Jehoahaz, who is removed from the throne by the Pharaoh after ruling for only three months (608). He is replaced by Jehoiakim, whom Jeremiah is quick to denounce as an evil king.

Chapter 23

This chapter is hard to date. It is typical of Jeremiah's prophecies and could apply at different times of his life.

Chapter 24

This chapter applies to the time of the exile of king Jehoiachin (597).

The best and the brightest are exiled to Babylon. Jeremiah pegs his hopes for the future on these exiles.

Chapter 25

We are now back to the time of King Jehoiakim. We are actually told the exact year. In 605 the Battle of Charchemish takes place, making Nebuchadnezzar the victor. Jeremiah's prophecies about the enemy from the north come true.

Chapter 26

We go back to the beginning of the reign of Jehoiakim (608-606). Jeremiah prophesies the destruction of the Temple and is put on trial for his life. He narrowly escapes execution. Another prophet, Uriah, prophesies the same thing and is put to death.

Chapters 27-28

We fast forward to 595, the time of King Zedekiah (the reference to Jehoiakim in 27:1 is erroneous). Jeremiah clashes with the prophet Hananiah, who predicts a quick return of the exiles from Babylon.

Chapter 29

Jeremiah sends a letter to King Jehoiachin and the exiled Judeans (c. 596-5), telling them to start a new life in Babylon, since it will take several decades before they return. Here Jeremiah begins to exert some influence on the exiles, who will return in due time and save Judaism.

Chapters 30-31

Prophecies of consolation follow here, showing Jeremiah having his prophecies recorded for future generations. This seems to be a composite text of different prophecies from different times, with the theme of redemption as the common denominator. Some of the prophet's most beautiful words appear here ("Rachel crying for her children.")

Chapters 32-35

We are now in the time of the siege of Jerusalem (587). This is the most harrowing time in the life of Jeremiah and his people. Yet it does not prevent him from buying a field in his native town of Anathoth as a show of faith in the future return.

Chapter 36

This chapter is out of chronological order. It goes back to the year 604 during the reign of Jehoiakim. Jeremiah writes a scroll of prophecies defying Jehoiakim's rebellion against Babylon. The king burns the scroll, eliciting a dire prophecy from Jeremiah.

Chapters 37-40

The tragic drama of the fall of Jerusalem unfolds in these chapters. Jeremiah spends part of that time in prison, but his life is spared by the victorious Babylonians.

Chapters 41-44

In the aftermath of the fall of Jerusalem, Gedaliah is appointed governor of the conquered province of Judah. He is assassinated by a member of the Judean royal family. Jeremiah, worn out with age, is forced by a group of Judeans to flee with them to Egypt. In Egypt, Jeremiah chastises the local Jewish residents who pursue idolatry.

Chapter 45

This short chapter dates back to the time of King Jehoiakim and contains words by Jeremiah to his scribe who seems to lose heart during that trying period in their lives.

Chapters 46-51

A string of prophecies against Judah's surrounding nations. None of them will escape divine retribution, above all Babylon.

Chapter 52

This final chapter is a prose narrative of the bitter end of King Zedekiah and his family, ending with the release of the exiled King Jehoiachin from Babylonian prison. It was most likely added to the book later on.

Chapter One

The Life and Mission of Jeremiah

1.

Why Jeremiah?

Let us begin with both the mystery and the reality of Jeremiah.

There is a prophet in the Hebrew Bible known as "Second Isaiah" because his prophecies are attached to the original book of Isaiah. His impact on Judaism and even more so on Christianity has been enormous. Yet we have no idea who he was, and he remains nameless to this day. We do know from reading his sublime poetry that he lived during the time of the return of the Judeans exiles from Babylonia to Jerusalem, the period in history following the time of Jeremiah. Some of his poems deal with God's so-called "suffering servant," a mysterious person who suffers for the sins of his generation and thus brings redemption to his people. To Jews, the suffering servant has symbolized the Jewish people, who are God's witnesses to the world and who have suffered for it. Christianity to this day believes the suffering servant is a foreshadowing of Jesus, through whose suffering the world is redeemed.

As I was doing my research for this book, one day I happened to look at one of the poems of the suffering servant, and I suddenly began to see something I had never seen before. The first seven verses of chapter 53, which indeed seem to describe Jesus, came into focus for me as a coded biography of the prophet Jeremiah. The mysterious poet-prophet managed to skillfully weave Jeremiah's life story into his text, holding up Jeremiah as the suffering servant of God who redeems his people. More on this in a later section of this book dedicated to Jeremiah's impact on Second Isaiah.

One of my Bible professors in graduate school, the late Dr. Samuel Sandmel, once referred to biblical scholarship as "detective work." Most of the biblical message is hidden rather than apparent, and needs to be decoded. This is particularly true in regard to the book of Jeremiah. Much of what he has to say is not

1

clearly or fully spelled out, and needs to be carefully pieced together. The chronology needs to be reestablished; layers of text have to be sifted through; small hints explored; parallel texts elsewhere in Scripture consulted; other ancient Near East records considered. In other words, we need to embark on a journey of exploration in the hope of discovering the real Jeremiah and understanding his life's work and his timeless message.

But there is another side to the Jeremiah story. The Bible, while containing a great deal of history, is not primarily a book of history. Rather, it is a book describing the spiritual odyssey of the human race with the story of one particular people at its center. From the time of Abraham to Moses to the early kings of Israel, historical data is either scarce or nonexistent. It all changes around the time of last kings of Israel and Judah. People and events described in the book of Jeremiah are firmly rooted in recorded history. In recent years, some major archeological discoveries have been made, including the Lachish Letters, first discovered in 1935, which verify historical events mentioned in the book of Jeremiah. In 1975, a clay seal impression bearing the signature of Jeremiah's personal scribe, Baruch ben Neriah was discovered in Israel, the first object ever found belonging to a biblical personality. In 2005 and again in 2008 a similar discovery was made of seal impressions of two counselors of the last king of Judah, who are mentioned in the book of Jeremiah as the ones who asked the king to execute Jeremiah for sedition. In short, the reality of Jeremiah, his contemporaries and his time is now being solidly established. Unlike other major biblical personalities, we no longer need to take Jeremiah strictly on faith. We can begin to study him as an integral part of our history.[1]

Who was Jeremiah?

No one in the Bible loved his people more than he did. Yet no one chastised them more harshly. He prophesied doom, and he cried. He cursed the day of his birth. He survived several attempts on his life while influencing the destiny of his people and of the entire human race during his long years of misery and suffering. Without him, Judaism may not have survived; Christianity and Islam may not have come into being.

In his day, the Jewish people ceased to exist as a sovereign nation. The religion of Israel was about to disappear. The pagan world was reigning supreme. The teachings of the Torah were about to be forgotten. As the remnants of Judah were driven into Babylonian exile, this man, now old and worn with age, was forced by some exiles to go with them down to Egypt, where he disappeared from the pages of history. His influence, however, continues to this day. At the most critical moment in world history, this great sufferer ensured the survival of his own people by showing them how to overcome exile, and in time he would inspire the founders of both Christianity and Islam. The three monotheistic civilizations can trace their roots to this man who lived in Jerusalem around 600 BCE.

No other prophet in the Bible provides a more detailed and intimate portrait of himself than Jeremiah. None, however, is more misunderstood. In the popular mind, Jeremiah is simply the long suffering prophet of gloom and doom. A Jeremiad—the English noun derived from his name—is a bitter lament. Jeremiah inhabits a space in the Bible between two other giants—Isaiah and Ezekiel, the first best known for his magnificent prophecy of the end of days, and the second for his vision of the resurrection of the dry bones. Between these two towering visionaries Jeremiah seems to cower and grovel. After many years of studying the Bible and, by my own admission, being partial to this particular, seemingly unhappy prophet, I have come to the conclusion that behind his bitter exterior, Jeremiah was an altogether different person. Far from being a passive messenger conveying God's dire prophecies, Jeremiah was a fearless social activist, a man of vision who understood that paganism was doomed, and who knew how to lay down a legacy of faith for the ages. Much of what he accomplished, which has deeply affected the course of world history, has remained unknown. Moreover, I now realize Jeremiah has a great deal to say to us today, at the tumultuous and uncertain start of the twenty-first century.

Jeremiah lived before, during, and after what was—until that time—the most catastrophic event in the history of ancient Israel, namely, the destruction of Jerusalem and the First Temple, and the end of the Davidic monarchy and of Jewish sovereignty. If history follows any laws, then the small nation of Israel had reached its end. Like so many other small nations of the time—Philistines, Edomites, Ammonites, Jebusites, Moabites, the list goes on and on—the people of Israel were now ready to leave the stage of history and never be heard from again. It is largely because of Jeremiah that the remnants of this small nation returned from Babylonian exile some seventy years later, built the Second Temple, and returned yet a second time in the twentieth century—something unparalleled in all of human history.

To most Jewish scholars, Jeremiah is only interested in his own people, and is only concerned with other nations insofar as they affect this people. To Christian scholars, Jeremiah is the prophet who foreshadows Christianity, especially when he speaks about the "New Covenant," which can also be translated from Hebrew as the "New Testament." The fact remains that in his first encounter with God, Jeremiah is told, "Behold, I appoint you today over nations and kingdoms." Later on, as he reaches the end of his prophetic career, Jeremiah addresses the nations of his time not in terms of their attitude towards his people, but in terms of their own particular fate.

Clearly, the poetic and often cryptic language of a Hebrew prophet writing centuries ago can be variably construed and misconstrued. Moreover—and this is true about almost all scholars regardless of their religious or ethnic background—the discipline of biblical scholarship, like all academic disciplines, calls for rational and dispassionate analysis of the available data. Yet the Bible, particularly in the utterances of the prophets, is far from dispassionate. Jeremiah in particular is a very emotional prophet-poet, and understanding his emotional-poetic temper is critical to deciphering his message. This to a large extent may account for the fact that this particular prophet has been so misunderstood by biblical scholars and commentators for so long.

Although I confess to a healthy bias regarding my own Jewish heritage, it is my intention to look at Jeremiah in the broadest way possible, not only from the Jewish point of view, and not only using the analytical method, but rather by delving into the emotional content of the book and drawing my own conclusions without taking sides and without prejudging.

2.

God Speaks to Jeremiah

Jeremiah tells us that God called him forth to be a prophet while he was still in his mother's womb:

> Before I created you in the womb I knew you,
> And before you were born I consecrated you
> As a prophet to the nations. (1:4)

Jeremiah, however, was not born a prophet. A descendant of generations of priests, he was destined from birth to serve as a priest. He would not begin to pursue his prophetic calling until his early manhood, and it would take years before he became recognized as a true prophet.

He tells us nothing about his father. We only know from the opening verse of the book that his father's name was Hilkiah the priest. We also know that this was the name of the High Priest in Jerusalem at that time. Was it the same person? Some classical Jewish commentators believe it was (see David Kimhi's commentary on Jeremiah 1:1). Current biblical scholars hesitate to make this assertion. But there are some good reasons to believe that they are indeed one and the same, as we shall soon see.

His family's history in the town of Anathoth dates back at least three centuries, to the time of the High Priest Abiathar who was banished to that priestly town by King Solomon. What was Anathoth like in the time of Jeremiah? Today it is an Arab village close to the northernmost Jewish suburbs of Jerusalem, called Anata. It is part of the West Bank, which consists for the most part of barren, rocky hills (one of the main sources of livelihood in Anata is stone cutting). The barrenness of the landscape is attributed mainly to the Ottoman (Turkish) Empire, which occupied this land from 1516 until 1917, exactly four hundred years. The Ottomans were far from enlightened rulers. They mistreated their Arab coreligionists and abused the land they lived on. Trees were cut down for military use and the land was laid waste. Today it is hard to believe that in Jeremiah's time the hill country north of Jerusalem was lush and wooded, and that the woods were home to wild life that included bears (see story of Elisha and the two she-bears), and further to the south there were lions and leopards (see story of Samson and the lion, and also the frequent references to lions and other predators by many of the prophets). It was fertile land that grew wheat, grapes, figs and olives, and provided grazing for cattle, sheep and goats. It was, indeed, a land flowing with milk and honey, and in times of peace its inhabitants dwelled "under their vines and their fig trees." (Micah 4:4)

In this idyllic countryside setting Jeremiah first saw the light of day and spent his childhood. It was most probably a happy childhood, as he would remain attached to his hometown for the rest of his long life and never develop a taste for the city life of Jerusalem, where he would spend most of his adult life.

Jeremiah the child was close to nature and took great interest in the rich plant and animal life around him. He was meditative, reclusive, and observant, as befitted someone who would become not only a great prophet but also a great poet. Nature fascinated him. Before he discovered God in history, he found God in nature. His very first encounter with God occurs as he observes an almond tree in bloom. This encounter, described in two short verses, speaks volumes. The almond tree is the first tree to bloom in the early spring in the Land of Israel. Winter is not quite over when this tree bursts with white and pink blossoms, glistening between raindrops and bright sunshine. There is a spiritual quality to it, and the sages of the Talmud called it the "New Year of the Trees." Nature is renewing itself, and God's creation—which according to Jewish belief is renewed every day—comes to mind. The sight of a blossoming almond branch fascinates Jeremiah the child. He is lost in reverie as he gazes upon the bright whiteness of the flowers, and for the first time he finds himself communing with the divine. Words begin to take shape in his mind. The Hebrew word for almond tree is *sha'ked*. He wonders: Why is this particular, early blossoming tree called *sha'ked*? Language is more than a human invention. It is a gift from God. We use human language to pray and talk to God. The world is created by the spoken word ("and God said.") Christianity believes that "In the beginning was the word." And the same idea is found in Greek philosophy. Surely there is a hidden message in the word *sha'ked*.

And suddenly Jeremiah receives his first divine insight. He knows that every Hebrew noun is derived from a verb root consisting of three letters, in this case sh-k-d. This particular Hebrew verb denotes "to be intent" on or "to be watchful." In other words, God is directly involved in the ongoing work of creation, which applies to the universe in general and to the affairs of God's creatures in particular. As the first sign of spring appears, it conveys to him this direct message, which is critical to his vocation as a prophet. From now on, nature becomes the tablet upon which he will receive divine messages. From now on, he will see the world with new eyes. And throughout his prophetic career he will continue to find in nature similes and metaphors for his prophecies.[2]

The child Jeremiah is startled as he feels a hand touching his lips. He looks up. There is no one around. He is alone. The sun is shining above the almond tree. He then realizes he is not alone. From now on, he will never be alone. He waits to hear the voice. And then the voice speaks.

It is at this point that we begin to raise questions. How can the human ear hear the voice of God? What does God sound like? How can a child gazing at an almond tree suddenly be conversing with God? Why did it happen in those days and not in our time?

The Bible is very emphatic about this phenomenon. An earlier example is that of the boy Samuel who serves the old priest Eli at the temple in Shiloh (where the Holy Ark was kept before it was transferred to Jerusalem) when suddenly he hears the voice of God:

> And the boy Samuel ministered to Adonai before Eli.
> And the word of the Almighty was rare in those days.
> There was no frequent vision. On that day Eli was lying
> in bed and his eyes dimmed, and could not see.
> The light of God had not yet gone out. And Samuel was
> lying in the temple of Adonai where the Ark of God was.
> And God called out to Samuel, and Samuel said, Here I am.
> And he ran to Eli and said to him, Here I am, for you have
> called me. And he said, I did not call, go lie down. And he
> went and he lay down. And Adonai called out again and
> said, Samuel. And Samuel stood up and went to Eli and said,
> Here I am, for you have called me. And he said, I did not
> call you, my son, go lie down.
> And Samuel had not yet known God, and the word of God
> had not yet been revealed to him.
> And God called Samuel for the third time, and he stood up and
> went to see Eli and said, Here I am, for you have called me.
> And Eli understood that God was addressing the boy.
> And Eli told Samuel, Go lie down, and if you are addressed
> again you will say, Speak, O God, for your servant is listening.
> (I Samuel 3:1-10)

This may be the most revealing passage in the Bible as to the way God communicates with human beings. It is not as dramatic as God addressing Moses from the burning bush, or Elijah hearing the "still small voice" after the storm in the desert. But it provides some specific and most revealing data not found elsewhere. Most importantly, it answers the question, what does God sound like? Clearly, to Samuel God sounded like his master, the priest Eli. When he heard God's voice, he mistook it for Eli's voice—not once but three times. Moreover, Samuel hears God's voice while lying in bed, either asleep or half awake. Finally, once Eli realizes his apprentice is receiving a divine message, he instructs him how to address God, which means that an established formula existed as to how to address God when one hears God's voice.

This phenomenon of hearing God's voice existed in Judaism for an uninterrupted period of over one thousand years, if we count back to the time of Moses, or nearly two thousand years if we go back to the time of Abraham. The above passage from the book of Samuel makes it clear that at certain times the voice was heard with greater frequency than in other times. Samuel lived after the period of the Judges, when lawlessness among the twelve tribes of Israel was the order of the day ("Each person did what he or she saw fit to do" [Judges 21:25]). It was a low point in the spiritual history of Israel, and the voice of God was not often heard. This will change in the days of Samuel and thereafter. At the end of the biblical period, Jewish prophecy comes to an end. Prophecy in other nations and religions goes beyond the scope of the present discussion. In Judaism, an edict was pronounced by the sages of the Talmud, who were the spiritual heirs to the sages of the Bible, stating: "One does not heed a divine voice." The divine voice, or *bat kol* in Hebrew, literally a nuance of a voice, was the divine message prophets received. It was determined that prophecy was a one-time phenomenon, albeit covering a very long period of time, never to be repeated again.

But when all is said and done, when Jeremiah feels the hand of God touching his lips, and when he hears the voice of God, he is communicating something to us that is not in the realm of our tactile or auditory human experience. The Bible is full of anthropomorphisms and anthropopathisms (human attributes and feelings believed to be found beyond the human realm). Jewish sages throughout time have been aware of this problem, and have made it clear that the Bible had to speak "in human language" in order for people to understand the divine message. Thus, God does not speak with a human voice, but rather *appears* to be speaking. God did not speak to Samuel the way Eli would, but Samuel at a young age began to have divine insights, and those insights were verbalized in his mind. The same holds true in regard to Jeremiah and all the other prophets. In the final analysis, what makes them prophets is not the physical act of hearing the voice of God, but their ability to understand, in the words of the prophet Micah, "what God wants us to do" (Micah 6:8). If we all shared their ability to understand, there would be no need for prophets and for divine revelation. God spoke to them, and through them, because people failed to understand—to borrow again the words of Micah— "what is good, and what Adonai demands of us." And nowhere is this sad truth more urgent and more striking than in the prophecies of Jeremiah.

3.

God's Unwilling Servant

We return to the boy Jeremiah on that sunny pre-spring day in his native town. He hears God's voice telling him of his mission. He is startled. Once he overcomes his fright, he says, "Aha, Adonai God, I don't know how to speak, for I am but a young boy."

The exclamation "Aha" denotes fear and anxiety. God reassures Jeremiah by touching his lips and telling him not to fear anyone, for from now on God will be speaking through him. And here God makes it clear that Jeremiah is empowered as God's messenger to prophesy not only to Israel but also to the nations. He will be addressing his own people and all people regarding their inescapable fate, a fate of destruction, uprooting, and loss, and at the same time a fate of eventual rebuilding and replanting.

There is no indication that Jeremiah, who is now in his early or mid-teens, started prophesying from the moment he first heard God's voice. More likely, he went through a period of apprenticeship that lasted into his twenties. He tells us that the word of God first came to him in the thirteenth year of the reign of King Josiah (628 BCE), at which time he was a young boy, and he proceeds to relate the episode of the almond tree. The next several years of his life, leading up to his first public appearance in Jerusalem[3] are not accounted for anywhere in the book, leaving a critical gap for us to fill up.

What happened to Jeremiah during those formative years?

As a student for the priesthood, Jeremiah studied the laws, the lore, and the history of his people, which in biblical times were all grouped under the term Torah, or teaching, and which later on became incorporated into what we call the Bible, literally "the books." The role of the priest was not only to offer sacrifices at God's altar, but also to instruct the people and preserve the faith. The priests were the religious authorities of their time. Six centuries later, after the destruction of the Second Temple in 70 CE, when the sacrificial cult abruptly came to an end, they would be replaced by the sages of the Mishnah and the Talmud, known as rabbis, a title that would remain in effect to this day.

What has become clear in recent years, after more than a century of intense study, analysis, and explorations by countless Christian and Jewish scholars, is that during the first half of Jeremiah's lifetime the most important concepts of the Hebrew Bible, namely, the unity of God, God's laws, the covenant between God and Israel, and the beginning of the process of assembling the Bible as a cohesive body of writings, began to take shape. It becomes clear that the young Jeremiah did much more than study an established text called the Torah. He actually participated in the process of shaping the key concepts of the Torah, and under his influence the Torah would begin to take hold among the Jews as the divine message from God to Israel, and would eventually replace the Temple and the sacrificial cult as the rock upon which Judaism stands.

Unlike other students of the priesthood his age, Jeremiah must have approached the study of Torah from the vantage point of his prophetic vocation, which made the text appear to him in a new light. His classmates learned by rote, while he filtered the text through the imperative handed him on that sunny day before the almond tree. This imperative made him examine each word carefully, as if his life depended on it. So while still in his early teens, he became serious and aloof, and would rarely take part in the youthful games his friends played. When his father tried to encourage him to be more like other boys his age, he would reply that he felt he had a special mission to fulfill, and needed much time for thought and reflection. At one point he told his parents he did not plan to become a priest, but rather preferred to wait for God to enlighten him as to what his mission was. His father did not take kindly to this manifestation of disobedience. He reminded him that he was the scion of many generations of priests, going back to the times of Moses and Aaron, and that it was the will of God for him to continue this unbroken chain of the tradition.

Jeremiah knew he was answering to a higher authority, but at the same time he knew the commandment, "Honor your father and your mother." This was the beginning of his lifelong conflict, having to choose between human and divine authority. It was also the beginning of the process of his estrangement from his father. Later on, when he began to chastise the priests for their lack of understanding and loyalty to the Torah, out of respect for his father he would never single him out or mention him by name.

Around the time Jeremiah was born, an eight-year-old prince of the house of David ascended the throne in Jerusalem. His name was Josiah. During the short reign of his father, Amon, and the much longer reign of his grandfather, Manasseh, the Kingdom of Judah became submerged in pagan practices, customs and beliefs. As Josiah grew up, he became determined to do away with those pagan practices. But it would be too little too late. It would become Jeremiah's life's mission to combat paganism in the hope of saving Judah from its dire fate. Jeremiah would lose this lifelong battle. But posthumously, he would win the war.

What exactly was paganism?

The term, clearly, is pejorative. However, not everything about what we call pagan religions was bad. Thus, for example, the Hebrew Ten Commandments have their origins in the much older code of the pagan Babylonian king Hammurabi, and the idea of one deity ruling the universe first originated in pagan Egypt before the time of Moses. Nevertheless, there is a fundamental difference between Hebrew monotheism and the religions we call pagan. Monotheism is the belief in a force beyond nature, a force that created nature, continues to control it, and actively imposes upon it laws of justice and mercy. Paganism, on the other hand, is the worship of natural forces, such as the sun, the moon, the earth, stars and so on, as though natural forces have a will of their own that can affect human affairs. Paganism is invariably polytheistic, worshiping a pantheon of so-called gods. It goes a step further in creating visible images of such gods, known as idols. In the pagan worship-system, human authority, such as the king, may have divine attributes. Finally, paganism, according to the biblical author, often resorts to immoral practices to please or appease the gods, and engages in such activities as divination, future-telling, necromancy, and so on. It should be pointed out that the biblical author goes to extremes describing paganism as cruel and corrupt belief systems that practice extreme rituals such as human sacrifice and ritual prostitution. Little evidence, however, has been found in the explorations and the study of ancient Near East religions of such practices, with very few exceptions. Rather, it appears that more often than not the Bible in portraying paganism in such harsh terms to make the point that there is a fundamental difference between Hebrew monotheism and paganism, in that the first leads to moral behavior while the second leads to immorality, particularly when practiced by those committed to the belief in the one God. Thus, the Ten Commandments, the cornerstone of biblical faith, begin with the oneness of God and the prohibition of believing in other gods and making physical images of the divine, and continue with God's fundamental moral commandments.

According to biblical belief, God first revealed himself to one person, namely, Abraham, who became the founder of a new nation known as Israel. It was God's intention to bring the knowledge of God to all the nations through Abraham and his descendants. During Abraham's lifetime and for centuries thereafter, however, the "families of the earth"—as humankind is referred to in the Bible—continued to practice idolatry, with all its attendant implications of finding divine attributes in nature; of not asserting human freedom while succumbing to a ruler with alleged divine qualities or rights; of failing to live by the biblical ethical code; and of being guided by superstitions. During those centuries, the small nation of Israel strove to practice a religion without idols, worshiping an invisible, intangible God, the kind of religion that made its neighbors wonder whether those odd people had any religion at all.

From a pragmatic standpoint, the people of Israel had cut themselves off culturally, socially, politically, and in every other way from the rest of the world. How could they argue persuasively that the whole world was wrong, and only they—a small nation who, in the words of the pagan prophet Balaam, "dwelled alone and was not counted among the nations," were right?

It should, therefore, come as no surprise that monotheism was not able to fully take root among the descendants of Abraham during the entire period of the monarchy. It was so monumental an idea, centuries ahead of its time; it went against the grain of the great civilizations of its time—from ancient Egypt and Babylonia to the first two great Western civilizations—Greece and Rome. It took incredible courage and stamina to be a monotheist in the time of Moses or David or Jeremiah. It was hardly something an entire nation could embrace and sustain.

We are told that the first monotheistic leader of what was to become the people of Israel was Moses. From the moment Moses receives the call to make God known to his people and defy the Pharaoh he is overwhelmed by the task, and elicits the help of his brother, Aaron. Moses becomes the prototype of the prophet, while Aaron becomes the prototype of the priest. Both are charged with the mission of implementing and preserving the belief in the one God and the adherence to God's law. This places an awesome responsibility on the two brothers, and since both are only human, they both fail to fully execute their mission. Moses' failure is not nearly as grave as Aaron's. Moses simply loses his temper at the people at one point, when God tells him to strike the rock and bring forth water, and does not follow God's exact order, for which he is punished by being forbidden to enter the Promised Land. Aaron, on the other hand, succumbs to the people's wishes to erect a golden calf when Moses is away receiving the tablets of the law. By doing so, Israel's first high priest according to the story in Exodus greatly angers God, and his life is spared only because of his brother's intercession.

After the twelve tribes of Israel settle in the Promised Land, the need for a king who would unify them into one nation that can defend itself becomes imperative. The person charged with this task is the prophet Samuel, who is also a priest and a judge. Samuel is painfully aware of the ethical and spiritual problems that would arise from establishing a monarchy. As a political entity, a monarchy follows the laws of man rather than the laws of God. Israel's uniqueness was not political, but rather spiritual. Once a political leader, namely, a king, became the supreme leader of all the people, the spiritual leaders, namely, the priests and the prophets, became subservient to this secular leader. And so Samuel anoints Israel's first king, Saul, not merely as a political leader, but also as a spiritual leader, whose authority comes directly from God. As one can expect, Saul soon fails to fulfill such a lofty mission. He disobeys God's command (transmitted through Samuel) to destroy Amalek, Israel's historical enemy, and loses God's favor. In his despair, he undertakes a secret journey to consult the woman of En-Dor, who conjures up for him the spirit of the dead prophet Samuel, only to find out that his own end is near.

Saul's successor, David, become's God's favorite (the name David in Hebrew is derived from the word beloved). While not a paragon of virtue, David nevertheless is a fervent believer in God, and remains to this day the king who is closest to God, hence the precursor or progenitor of the future messiah.

Paganism, however, returns to Israel in a big way during the closing years of the long reign of David's son, Solomon. While Solomon is called the wisest of men, he fails in two areas, both of which are frowned upon by the God of Israel. He increases his military power more than necessary, specifically by acquiring many horses and, worse yet, he takes hundreds of wives, many of them from foreign stock. The main reason for this excessive polygamy is political rather than personal. Each political alliance and conquest brings in new wives. Along with those multinational wives, Solomon's capital, Jerusalem, sees the arrival of foreign pagan religions. And so, ironically, the king who builds God's Holy Temple, is also the king who lets pagan religions take residence in God's city.

Solomon's failure to adhere to and ensure the continuity and the inviolability of his ancestors' faith is perhaps the great tragedy of ancient Israel. Here was the great golden moment in time for Israel to establish its covenantal relationship with God, but it was squandered. The subsequent history of the monarchy, which splits in two after Solomon's death and comes to an end in Jeremiah's time, is a history of steady decline.

During the two centuries of the divided kingdom, and in the century following the fall of the Northern Kingdom in 722 BCE, a few kings make attempts to fight paganism. One such king is Josiah's great-grandfather, Hezekiah. He begins the process of removing the pagan places of worship, but his reform is short-lived. His son, Manasseh, does not share his father's vision of returning to the God of Israel. He lives in the moment, and his moment in time is one of conforming to the wishes of the ruling nations of the day, and reintroducing their pagan rituals and observances to his kingdom. He goes so far as to "pass his son through the fire," a pagan practice considered an abomination, and is guilty of abusing his power by putting many innocent people to death. This was the order of the day during the fifty-five years of his rule, as well as the two years of the rule of his son, Amon.

This brings us to the first king Jeremiah knew, namely, Josiah. Even as a young teenager, this child-king, following in the footsteps of his great grandfather, Hezekiah, made the last brave attempt in the history of the monarchy to restore his people to their God. Most likely, he restores the authority of the Temple priests and brings disenfranchised priests from places like Anathoth to the capital, including Jeremiah's father, Hilkiah, who becomes the high priest. He orders Hilkiah to undertake a major restoration of the Holy Temple, which had been neglected for nearly six decades during the reign of Josiah's father, Amon, and his grandfather, Manasseh, and was in an advanced state of disrepair.

Hilkiah undertakes his task with great dispatch. He takes full inventory of all the offerings and the money collected from the people, engages craftsmen such as stonemasons and carpenters, and personally inspects the precincts of the Temple. In one of the chambers he discovers a dusty scroll that had been deposited there presumably by some priests who were out of favor with the king of their time (most likely Manasseh), and was kept out of public view. It is anyone's guess whether the scroll was discovered accidentally, or whether it was deliberately brought out by Hilkiah who knew about its existence. One does sense here a priestly design to bring this particular scroll to the attention of the young king, knowing full well that it would enhance his reformist zeal and bring about a change of heart regarding Israel's covenant with God and the rejection of idolatrous practices.

We learn about these events from the Second Book of Kings, chapters 22-23. The text refers to the scroll as "the book of the Torah," presumably hitherto unknown. All evidence points to sections from the book of Deuteronomy, which is in essence a recap of the first four books. While authorship of this book is attributed to Moses himself, there is little doubt that many hands account for its final shape, and it is widely believed that it is precisely at this time, during Jeremiah's youth, that the book was assembled and preserved in much the same way we know it today. As we turn later to the prophetic message of Jeremiah, we will see how dominant the text of Deuteronomy is in his teachings.

Hilkiah gives the newly found scroll to the king's scribe, Shaphan, who reads it and agrees to bring it to the attention of the king. Here again one gets the impression Hilkiah and Shaphan had carefully planned this presentation, since they do not inform the king about the scroll outright, but rather arrange for Shaphan to report to the king about the status of the fundraising for the restoration work, at which point Shaphan "happens" to mention to the king the scroll Hilkiah has found.

As expected, the king orders Shaphan to read him the scroll. After Shaphan is done reading, we hear that:

> When the king had heard the words of the book
> of the law, he rent his clothes. And the king
> commanded Hilkiah the priest, and Ahikam
> the son of Shaphan, and Achbor the son of Michaiah,
> and Shaphan the scribe, and Asahiah a servant of
> the king, saying, Go and inquire of Adonai for me,
> and for the people, and for all Judah, concerning
> the words of this book that is found: for great is
> the wrath of Adonai that is kindled against us,
> because our fathers have not hearkened to the
> words of this book, to do according to all that is
> written concerning us. (II Kings 22:11-13)

Rending one's clothes is a sign of mourning. The king reacts as though someone had just died. Most likely, he is reacting to curses in Deuteronomy that would befall those who break the divine law, which implies death. He must be thinking that those curses are about to befall some people he knows. He orders his servants to go and inquire of Adonai as to what happens next, which means speaking to a recognized prophet who is believed to know God's will. He then mentions "our fathers," alluding to the time of Amon and Manasseh, when the laws of the Torah were ignored and violated, which is bound to lead to dire consequences for their offspring.

The king's men turn to Huldah, the wife of Shallum, the keeper of the king's wardrobe, who is the closest recognized prophet they can find, and tell her what has happened. Here the Sages of the Talmud raise the question why they did not turn to Jeremiah, a much more prominent prophet of that time. The answer, quite simply, is that the young Jeremiah was not yet a recognized prophet, and did not have the ear of the king's court.

Huldah hears them out and replies:

> Thus says Adonai, Behold, I will bring evil upon this place,
> and upon its inhabitants, even all the words of
> the book that the king of Judah has read. Because they
> have forsaken Me, and have burned incense to other
> gods, that they might provoke My anger with all
> the works of their hands; therefore My wrath shall
> be kindled against this place, and shall not be
> quenched. But to the king of Judah who sent you
> to inquire of Adonai, thus shall you say to him,
> Thus says Adonai God of Israel, the words
> which you have heard: Because your heart was tender,
> and you have humbled yourself before Adonai,
> when you heard what I spoke against this place,
> and against its inhabitants, that they should become
> a desolation and a curse, and have rent your clothes,
> and wept before me; I also have heard you,
> says Adonai. Behold, therefore, I will gather you to
> your fathers, and you shall be gathered into your grave
> in peace; and your eyes shall not see all the evil which
> I will bring upon this place. . . . (II Kings 22:16-20)

In other words, King Josiah had redeemed himself by showing true repentance, and therefore was not going to be punished. But his people, after years of idolatrous practices, were beyond redemption and would be punished.

There is no doubt that this prophecy made a deep impression on the young Jeremiah. He will quote from it at least on two different occasions during his long prophetic career (1:16, 19:4). And as the young king begins his all-out war against idolatry, Jeremiah, the prophet-in-training, enters his great spiritual crisis that will accompany him for the rest of his life. The crisis will stem from the dichotomy of the great hope born of Josiah's renewal of the covenant on the one hand, and the dire prediction of Huldah on the other. After what Huldah had to say, one could only hope against hope.

Josiah proceeds with his reform. One can only marvel at the incredible scope of this reform, which seeks to undo three centuries of idolatrous practices in Jerusalem and the rest of the land, dating back to the time of King Solomon. First, the king assembles the entire people in front of the restored temple, and reads the newly found book of the Torah to the assemblage:

> The king stood by the pillar and made a covenant
> before Adonai, to follow Adonai, keep His
> commandments, His decrees, and His statutes,
> with all his heart and with all his soul, to perform
> the words of this covenant that were written in this book.
> All the people joined in the covenant. (II Kings 23:3)

This text quotes almost verbatim from the book of Deuteronomy, the book Josiah reads to the people. What follows here is an all-out attack on idolatry that must have taken months if not years, at the end of which all traces of idolatrous worship were removed from the realm. The first to go were the two gods that had been most common throughout the ancient Near East, namely, the Baal and his wife, the Asherah (or Astarte or Ishtar, depending on which ancient culture is involved). Those gods of fertility dated back to the ancient Canaanites or before, and remained a powerful presence through the ancient world until the end of the biblical period. Along with them went a host of gods representing the sun, the moon, the constellations, and all "the hosts of heaven," including the Queen of Heaven (akin to or same as the Asherah), which was a favorite of Judean women throughout Jeremiah's lifetime.[4]

Next came the high places and the gates where pagan worship took place. Those places were defiled and destroyed, and their priests discharged and even killed. From there the king turned to a place outside Jerusalem called Topheth, in the valley of Ben-Hinnom (from which the Hebrew word for hell was derived in post-biblical times), where children (including King Manasseh's son) were passed through the fire as a pagan practice known as a sacrifice to the Moloch (believed to be a deity, but more likely the name of the pagan practice itself), and destroyed it. Moreover, Josiah did away with all the mediums, wizards, teraphim (home idols that date back to the time of the Patriarchs), idols in general, and "all the abominations that were seen in the land of Judah and Jerusalem" (II Kings 23:24). In short, the purge was total, and was not only confined to Judah, but also extended to Samaria, which had belonged to the Northern kingdom, where the king destroyed the high place at Bethel which had been erected by the wayward king Jeroboam son of Nebat, who had caused many in Israel to sin. Finally, Josiah destroyed all the places of worship outside Jerusalem, leaving the Holy Temple as the only legitimate place of worship for the God of Israel.

Next the king returned to Jerusalem and proclaimed a public observance of the feast of Passover as prescribed in the Book of the Covenant (another name for the book of Deuteronomy). Outwardly, the land had been purged and the people had returned to God.

But were the people's hearts also purged?

The great misfortune of being a prophet is being ahead of one's time, seeing what others do not see or do not wish to see, and as a result being at odds with one's contemporaries. What makes this misfortune even greater for Jeremiah is his passionate love for his people, and his admiration for the young king. And here something else must have happened, of which Jeremiah keeps silent, and we can only try to fill in the blanks. As Josiah rid Jerusalem and the countryside of all the pagan priests and reestablished the centrality and the supremacy of the Temple in Jerusalem, the priestly class in the city, and particularly the high priest, Hilkiah, must have felt triumphant. They were now convinced that no harm could befall Judah. Huldah was wrong. Now that the covenant with the God of Abraham had been renewed and firmly reestablished, the *shekhinah*, God's presence or indwelling had returned to the Holy Temple in God's holy city. Hilkiah, the overseer of the restoration of the Temple, must have been the happiest man in Judah.

His son, Jeremiah, however, did not share his feelings. What the young Jeremiah soon learned was that the reform was mostly an outward expression of the centralized cult of Jerusalem. People continued to engage in idol worshiping in the privacy of their homes. Worse yet, prophets were dispensing false prophecies, and priests were lax in upholding and teaching the law. When he brought all this to his father's attention, Hilkiah explained it away by arguing that after decades of laxity and waywardness, things could not change overnight. It would take time. One has to be patient and wait. It would all turn out for the best in the end.

Jeremiah, though young in years, knew better. (It reminds us of young Jews in Europe on the eve of World War Two. For years, and especially with Hitler's rise to power in Germany, the writing was on the wall for European Jews, but the older generation refused to believe it. It was mostly young people, and all too few at that, who heeded the message and left while there was still time.) Jeremiah did not see things getting better, only worse. And to judge from his confrontational behavior throughout his prophetic career, at one point he must have thundered out against his father and his other family members, most likely at some family gathering in Anathoth, and accused them of complicity and laxity, warning that God is watching and will not forgive.

One can hear his father, the high priest, reply through clenched teeth, making a supreme effort not to explode: If you know better than all of us, then go and live by yourself and let God take care of you. But don't come back and ask me to bail you out. From now on, you are on your own.

Jeremiah has now become a persona non grata in his native town. He finds a place for himself in Jerusalem, where he probably does odd jobs, working mainly as a tutor, having among his students a bright young member of the upper class, Baruch ben Neriah. He now becomes fully dedicated to his mission, and he receives his first divine charge.

4.

I Remember the Kindness of Your Youth

This is no longer the boy Jeremiah. He is now a young adult, his beard and his hair have grown long, and he roams the streets of Jerusalem, looking for places where people gather, trying to get their attention. There is a sense of complacency in the city. Judah's archenemy, Assyria, is on the decline, and does not pose a threat as she did in the past. Babylonia has not yet asserted herself, and Egypt is too busy with her own problems to be able to bother her neighbor to the north. King Josiah, now in his early thirties, is a righteous, God-fearing king. The priests are ministering at the Holy Temple, now restored to its former splendor. The people firmly believe no harm can befall their city, since God has returned to dwell in it, and no power in the world can defy the Almighty.

It is against this backdrop that Jeremiah begins to deliver his unpopular message. According to this message, God is not fooled by the smug, self-righteous Judeans. In fact, God feels let down, forsaken, and betrayed by the people he once saved from slavery, guided through the desert, and brought to a land flowing with milk and honey. Here is what God has sent me to tell you, Jeremiah says:

> I remember the kindness of your youth,
> The love of your betrothal,
> How you followed Me in the desert,
> In a land not sown. (2:2)

This gets the people's attention. This man is a real poet. What a beautiful way to describe their return to their God! So far so good. They are in full agreement with what this strange, unknown prophet has just said. They all know about the exodus from Egypt, the trek through the desert, and the conquest of the Land of Canaan. They also know about the covenant between God and Israel, which Jeremiah is likening to a marriage, and about its renewal by their beloved king, Josiah. And they are certainly very pleased when a prophet reaffirms what they already believe. But after a short pause, Jeremiah continues:

> Listen to the word of Adonai O House of Jacob
> And all the families of the House of Israel.
> Thus says Adonai: What wrong did your fathers
> Find in Me that they abandoned me
> And went after delusion and were deluded? (2:4-5)

Well, the prophet is not speaking about them, but about their forebears who, as is well known, had left their God and followed the idols of their neighbors. Surely this prophet will now begin to praise them for their return to the true faith and for having renewed the covenant. But Jeremiah is about to surprise them:

> I have brought you to this bountiful land
> To enjoy its fruit and its goodness
> And you have defiled My land
> And have made my possession an abomination.
> The priests did not ask themselves, Where is Adonai?
> And the teachers of the law did not know Me,
> And the leaders of the people rebelled against Me
> And the prophets prophesied by the Baal
> And followed useless gods.
> Therefore I will take you to task, says Adonai,
> And I will take your children's children to task. (2:7-9)

The message now becomes clear. In spite of the great reformation, there has been no change of heart among the people, or, for that matter, among their spiritual and political leaders. Yes, the Deuteronomic law has become the official law of the land, but only outwardly. The spirit of the law, the ethical teachings embodied in the Ten Commandment and all the other statutes and decrees of God's law, and the total prohibition of idolatry, are not being followed. The same people who come to the Holy Temple in Jerusalem to bring offerings to God, in the privacy of their homes continue to worship the Baal and the Queen of Heaven, and a host of other pagan deities.

Some people are thinking to themselves: What we do in the privacy of our homes is our business, no one else's. In public, we do what God commands us to do.

Jeremiah can tell what they are thinking. He responds:

> Just go to the Isles of Kitim and look,
> Send to Kedar and observe carefully,
> Was there ever anything like this? (2:10)

In other words, the pagan nations of the Greek isles (Kitim), or the nomadic tribes of the Arabian Desert (Kedar), though practicing idolatry, remain constant in their allegiance to their particular deities, while Israel betrayed their God by surreptitiously resorting to idolatrous practices. Indeed, they could not fool God. They could not hide their backsliding.

Huldah was wrong! Someone yells out, alluding to the dire prediction made by Huldah the prophet at the outset of King Josiah's reformation. God is with us, and while empires all around us are crumbling, Judah will continue to dwell forever and Jerusalem to all generations!

Not so, Jeremiah replies. Look what happened to the Northern Kingdom of Israel. For the past one hundred years, since her destruction at the hands of Assyria, she has remained desolate, her cities destroyed and without inhabitants, and lions roar in her forests. Was Israel any less favored by God than Judah? Was it not a free kingdom and a sister nation to Judah?

The crowd begins to disperse. They are not interested in what this new prophet has to say. They are busy people, and they have better things to do. Someone suggests that he go back to Anathoth and leave the people of Jerusalem alone.

Jeremiah does not give up. The mark of a true prophet is that he does not fold in the face of adversity. On the contrary, he becomes more determined to continue to deliver his message regardless of consequences. Jeremiah realizes that while he was not able to persuade his listeners to mend their ways, he did get their attention, and he did start them thinking. Deep down they knew he was right, but they were suppressing the truth. What he needed to do was dramatize God's message, deliver it in such a way that would force the people to face up to the truth and repent. Simple everyday language would not accomplish this goal. He must resort to eloquent poetic imagery, which he knew would make a deep impression on his listeners.

And so he keeps returning to the places of gathering, mainly the courtyards and the steps of the Temple, but also the markets and the inns, and he passionately pleads his case against idolatry and immorality:

> Be astonished, O heavens, at this,
> And be horribly afraid, be very desolate, says Adonai,
> For my people have committed two evils,
> They have forsaken Me, the fountain of living waters,
> And they have made themselves cisterns,
> Broken cisterns that can hold no water. (2:12-13)

God is the fountain of life, while the idols are man-made folly. How can people who for centuries now have come to know the living God put their trust in idols? Jeremiah asked this question twenty-six centuries ago, but it echoes throughout the ages, and continues to face humanity every day. We may not be worshiping the Baal and the Asherah any longer, but we worship power and money, the celebrities of the moment, human science, and other idols. Modern paganism has many faces, but it all comes back to the same thing: We keep losing sight of how insignificant we are in the greater scheme of things. Jeremiah goes on to say:

Thus says Adonai:
Let not the wise glory in his wisdom
And let not the mighty glory in his might,
And let not the rich glory in his wealth.
But let him glory who knows Me,
Who knows that I am Adonai,
Who does mercy and justice and
Righteousness in the land,
For this is what I want, says Adonai.   (9:22-23)

Jeremiah could not be more explicit. Overreliance on human knowledge, power, and wealth are tantamount to idol worshiping. They stand in direct opposition to the kind of behavior required of human beings, namely, the practice of mercy, justice, and righteousness.

What becomes clear is that the righteous King Josiah could only do so much. He could take action against foreign cults and idolatrous practices, but he could not wean the people from the habits of their fathers.

5.

The Enemy from the North

The people refuse to take responsibility for their idolatrous and immoral actions. Jeremiah's words fall on deaf ears. His eloquence and the vivid imagery of his admonitions are to no avail. The people and their leaders are completely caught up in the politics of the moment and see no danger on the horizon. Jeremiah, on the other hand, understands that the lull during the shift of power across the borders of Judah is only short-lived. There cannot be a power vacuum for long. One of the new emerging powers is going to prevail, and unless his people and their leaders begin to accept this geopolitical reality, they are going to suffer the consequences. But who might the new enemy be?

When God first reveals Himself to Jeremiah, the prophet receives two signs. The first is the blossoming almond tree, which has been previously discussed. The second is a boiling pot with an opening presumably blowing smoke towards the north. This sign is taken by Jeremiah to mean that trouble will come to his land from the north.

Much has been written about "the enemy from the north." Who this particular enemy is remains one of the unsolved questions in this book. The prophet provides some vivid visions of the "kingdoms of the north," whose kings would come, presumably with their armies, and set their thrones at Jerusalem's gates and around her walls and in all the towns of Judah, implying a major siege that would result in the fall and destruction of the Judean kingdom. We are not given any specific names of those kingdoms. What history shows is that the enemy who eventually comes and lays siege to Jerusalem and brings an end to Jewish sovereignty is Babylonia. It has been argued that Babylonia is located east, rather than north of Judah, or, more precisely, northeast. What becomes clear is that Jeremiah, who is not given a clear message from God about Babylonia at this point, is aware of a general danger emanating from the north, or perhaps northeast. He does not limit it to one enemy, but rather talks about kingdoms in the plural. It is only after the battle of Carchemish, on the Euphrates River, in 605 BCE, in which Assyria and Egypt make a last attempt to contain Babylonia, that it becomes clear to Jeremiah that the generic "enemy from the north" is indeed the triumphant King Nebuchadnezzar (Jeremiah calls him Nebuchadrezzar) of Babylonia, and instead of talking about a vague "enemy from the north," he begins to talk specifically about the Babylonian king who would come and destroy Jerusalem.

Four years before the fateful battle of Carchemish, which put an end to the Assyrian Empire, the armies of Pharaoh Necho of Egypt marched through the coast of Judah northward to help Assyria stop the advance of the new power now emerging in the Near East, namely, Babylonia. King Josiah decided to stop the Egyptians from reaching their destination. He deployed his forces in the Valley of Jezreel, at Megiddo, a place conducive to stopping large armies with relatively small forces (as had happened in the battle of Deborah and Barak against Siserah in the time of the Judges). The Pharaoh asked Josiah to withdraw, since he had no quarrel with him and was heading north to Assyria. The king did not listen. Instead, we are told in II Chronicles 35:22, he rode to the battlefield wearing a disguise. Necho's archers (or perhaps Josiah's own archers) did not recognize him when he arrived in Megiddo, and killed him. We are further told in Chronicles:

> And Jeremiah lamented for Josiah, and all the singing men
> and the singing women spoke of Josiah in their lamentations,
> to this day; and they made them an ordinance in Israel,
> and behold, they are written in the lamentations.
> (II Chronicles 35:25)

As we learn from this passage, Josiah's untimely death was a national tragedy. To Jeremiah it was a personal blow. We also learn that by the end of Josiah's reign Jeremiah had become a recognized prophet, and that his poetic talent as a eulogizer was valued. But this must have given him little comfort, as he realized that the righteousness of Josiah was not going to be duplicated by his two sons, Jehoahaz and Jehoiakim, or his grandson, Jehoiachin, or his third son, Zedekiah. The Judeans were given one last chance to mend their ways during the benevolent reign of King Josiah, but they failed. From now on, for the next twenty-three years remaining to the Kingdom of Judah, and thereafter, Jeremiah will have to deal with unrepentant monarchs, prophesy to people who refuse to listen, and at the same time begin to lay the foundation for the future of his people, indeed, for the future of monotheism.

6.

Return, Ye Mischievous Children

During the waning years of the kingdom, following the death of Josiah, Jeremiah will fully emerge as God's voice to his people. His popularity will continue to decline, but his message will become ever more important. The remaining kings of Judah will all "do that which is evil in the eyes of Adonai," helping to precipitate the fall of their kingdom. Jeremiah will do everything he can to change their hearts, but in effect he will be preparing his people for the post-monarchic future.

Why did all of Josiah's heirs fail to follow in his footsteps?

The Bible makes it sound as if they chose to do evil when, in fact, there was more to it. It could well be that all four of them lacked the character and the courage of their predecessor. Furthermore, we know from our present day experience that good leaders are always scarce. But much of it also had to do with the political circumstances of their time. After the death of Josiah resulting from his confrontation with Pharaoh Necho, this ruler subjugated Judah, removed Jehoahaz, Josiah's heir, from the throne, and put Jehoiakim in his place. Thus, Josiah's sons did not enjoy the relative independence that their father experienced, which enabled him to assert himself and introduce a far-reaching religious reform. With subjugation, idolatry as well as immorality came back. Jehoiakim, in addition, was ill-tempered, and terrorized his people. His son, Jehoiachin, only ruled for three months when the Babylonians arrived in Jerusalem and deposed him as they carried out the first deportation of Judeans to Babylonia. His uncle, Zedekiah, took his place as the last king of Judah, and proved to be a weak, indecisive ruler who let his advisors decide for him and brought upon himself his own doom.

It is against this dismal political backdrop that Jeremiah continues his prophetic mission as he calls out to his people and their leaders:

> Return, ye mischievous children,
> And I will heal your mischief. (3:22)

One cannot help but marvel at the deep sense of divine paternal love and compassion towards Israel evoked by this prophet. Israel is mischievous, causing mischief. But the voice of God is a loving voice pleading with God's children: Come back, don't be afraid, I will heal you. This is but one of many examples of how the prophet experiences and explains the relationship between the people and their God. One of the great themes in world literature is the ingratitude of children towards their parents. King Lear comes to mind ("How sharper than a serpent's tooth it is to have a thankless child"). Also Balzac's Father Goriot and his ungrateful daughters ("When I became a father I understood God").

God created man as a creature endowed with free will. Man is free to do good or to do evil. Free will is a godlike attribute. But much of the time man makes the wrong choice. Like all the other prophets in the Bible, Jeremiah is aware of this grim reality of the human condition. But with Jeremiah it takes on a greater urgency, for he knows that the days of the kingdom are numbered, a great catastrophe is about to happen, and the people remain oblivious to it. His pain grows day by day as he realizes that things are going from bad to worse.

To fully appreciate Jeremiah's plight, it should be pointed out that God becomes both his surrogate father and his master, and the people become his surrogate children. Jeremiah is estranged from his own family and from his own priestly community of Anathoth. To make matters worse, God orders Jeremiah:

> You shall not take a wife,
> Neither shall you have sons and
> Daughters in this place. (16:2)

God goes on to explain that few of the young will survive the impending destruction. What is more likely here is that God wants Jeremiah to be totally committed to his mission to the exclusion of his own personal fulfillment. Thus he becomes God's exclusive emissary, and his people's paternal voice. It is small wonder that more than once he is driven to the brink of total despair. But he never relents in his commitment to his calling, for a true father never abandons his children. He remains God's mouthpiece to the bitter end.

7.

God's Unfaithful Wife

What is perhaps Jeremiah's very first publicly-spoken prophetic message also remains his most memorable and most striking one. It is so hauntingly beautiful it continues to echo through the ages:

> I remember the kindness of your youth,
> The love of your betrothal,
> How you followed Me in the desert,
> In a land not sown. (2:2)

Jewish mysticism centuries later will make a great deal of the male-female relationship between God and Israel, but the origins of this concept are found here. More precisely, they are found in one of Jeremiah's predecessors, the prophet Hosea, who lived in the Northern Kingdom about a century before the time of Jeremiah and a few years before the destruction of that kingdom, and from whom Jeremiah borrows ideas as well as style. To dramatize Israel's (that is, the Northern Kingdom) betrayal of God, Hosea marries (or rather is ordered by God to marry) a prostitute and has children with her. The children come to symbolize the betrayal of God by his people and foreshadow the coming destruction. Jeremiah applies this concept to the Southern Kingdom's (Judah) betrayal of God. He traces the idea of the marriage between God and the Hebrew tribes back to the beginning of the covenant relationship—the time of the Exodus, and likens the covenant to a marriage ceremony. Obviously, Judah did not learn her lesson, and is about to face the same fate as her northern counterpart. Jeremiah's spiritual disciple and heir, Ezekiel, exiled in Babylonia, will combine Hosea's and Jeremiah's concepts and tell a parable about two sisters, Oholah and Oholibah who represent the two kingdoms, both of whom prostitute themselves and betray their husbands, bringing destruction upon their children.

It is much easier to understand likening the relationship between God and Israel to that between children and parents ("Return, ye mischievous children"), or even to one child and a parent ("My beloved son Ephraim") than a marriage. What prompted Hosea and Jeremiah as well as Ezekiel to use wedlock as the key concept in explaining the covenant?

With Jeremiah, this metaphor seems to become almost an obsession. When he calls his people children, they are "mischievous children" (*banim shovevim*). But when he calls Israel (the Northern Kingdom) a disloyal wife or, worse yet, a prostitute, he names her Mischief (*meshuvah*). She left her husband, namely, God, and followed other gods, for which God her husband gave her a divorce. Now, according to the law in Deuteronomy (more on this later), God could not take her back as a wife, and she was destroyed. And now her sister, whom the prophet calls "Judah the Traitor," is doing the same.

Jeremiah goes on to describe in great graphic detail how Judah the faithless wife prostitutes herself in every possible venue, on every hill and in every valley, making love to trees and stones (3:6), turning the whole land into a defiled place. Thus, prostitution and paganism become one and the same.

The most obvious explanation for associating paganism with prostitution is the presence of cultic prostitutes in pagan temples and places of worship in biblical times. In fact, the name for such a prostitute in the Bible, *k'desha*, is derived from the Hebrew root k-d-sh, meaning holy. We read in Deuteronomy: "There shall not be a *k'desha* from among the daughters of Israel" (23:18). One of the cornerstones of monotheism is the rejection of such practices. Recent scholarship, however, has cast doubt on the proliferation of such practices in the ancient Near East.

There may be another, more compelling reason for this metaphor, which is supported by some internal analysis of the prophecies and the prose narrative of the book of Jeremiah, and by some archeological evidence of recent years. I am referring to the worship of the Asherah (also Astarte, Ishtar etc.) in both Israel and Judah, under the name of the Queen of Heaven.[5] As was mentioned before, the worship of this goddess, especially among Hebrew women, was widespread during Jeremiah's lifetime, and long before. Jeremiah goes to great length to decry the worship of the Queen of Heaven, as a singular abomination. We are told that after the destruction of Jerusalem, when Jeremiah is forced to go down into exile to Egypt, he finds out that Hebrew women already living in Egypt also worship the Queen of Heaven (44:15-20) as they did back in Israel and Judah. When he reprimands them for doing so, their husbands mock him by saying that when they stopped worshipping her back home, it did not prevent God from destroying their city and exiling them, and now that they have returned to worship her, once again they are safe and prosperous.

Recent archeological discoveries include an inscription dating to the time of the prophet Hosea (8th century BCE), in which one Hebrew greets another "in the name of Yahweh and his Asherah."[6]

The implication is clear: Even as for idol-worshipping Hebrews the Asherah was the goddess-wife of the Baal, the Queen of Heaven was believed to be the wife of Adonai. To people like Hosea or Jeremiah, for whom God transcended human attributes and certainly human sexuality, this must have been the worst form of idolatry, turning God into an equivalent of the Baal. It may well be that this is what compelled Hosea as well as Jeremiah and Ezekiel to go to such great lengths to convey the idea that the God of Israel, unlike pagan gods, does not have a wife, simply because God has no gender and no physical attributes. Jeremiah likens the covenant between God and the people of Israel to a marriage to remind his people that God does not have a supernatural wife or a wife of any kind, rather a symbolic relationship with the people of Israel whose purpose it is to spread the knowledge of the true God among the people of the earth as God has promised Abraham. God therefore looks upon this relationship as a most sacred and critical contract. Breaking this contract is the highest form of betrayal of God possible, and therefore carries dire consequences.

It is against this backdrop of betrayal and prostitution that Jeremiah's first prophecy regarding his people, describing the early days of God's covenant with Israel in such rapturous and rhapsodic language is so compelling. At the end of his career, when he begins to offer consolation to the exiles who have been sorely tried and punished, the female image changes to the "daughter of Zion," the "virgin of Israel," once again a chaste woman, daughter, wife, mother, "Rachel crying for her children, refusing to be consoled."

8.

Is Jeremiah the First Jew?

Harsh as it is, Jeremiah fully accepts God's will. While his life seems to be in constant turmoil, and while he seems to go from one emotional crisis to the next, his faith is unwavering, and he is completely clear as to what his mission is. As we read his dire prophecies, full of exhortations and admonitions, we find ourselves facing an angry and unforgiving prophet. But when we look closer we begin to realize that there is a subtext here that transcends the immediate message. What makes this subtext of utmost importance is the fact that while the battle for the souls of his contemporaries—even though he continues to fight it— is already lost, the message of the subtext will prove crucial in the long run. In it, Jeremiah is preparing his people for their enduring monotheistic future.

In other words, the character and the core beliefs of post-biblical Judaism begin to take shape in the work and personality of the man from Anathoth. This brings us to what may appear to be a startling conclusion: while Abraham may be considered the first Hebrew, Jeremiah is the first Jew. Until Jeremiah's time, the people of Israel are Hebrews. After him, they become Jews. His life and teachings are responsible for this transformation.

What is the difference between Hebrew and Jew?

Hebrew is an ethnic term. It is first applied to a small nomadic people who migrated from Mesopotamia to Canaan in the nineteenth century BCE. We first hear it mentioned during the time of the patriarchs. When the wife of Joseph's Egyptian master, Potiphar, tries to seduce the young slave, she refers to him as "a Hebrew man" (Genesis 39:14). The ancient Hebrews were a Semitic people related to other ethnic groups in the Ancient Near East such as the Arabs. Their language was derived from a common Semitic origin, of which Arabic is an earlier example. Abraham is believed to be the common ancestor of this people, but from the very beginning the Hebrews were divided into tribes, at least twelve in number, and the tribal loyalties remained strong up to the time of Jeremiah. What the tribes had in common was the belief in the one God of the Universe, and in the covenant between God and the tribes of Israel. The pivotal event in the history of the tribes is their liberation from Egyptian bondage that results in the giving of the law at Sinai and the conquest of the Promised Land. But what becomes clear in the pronouncements of the biblical prophets, is that the history of the Hebrew tribes is not one of loyalty to the one God and to God's law, but rather a wavering between monotheism and paganism. During the five centuries of the Hebrew monarchy, which ends at the time of Jeremiah, the covenant between God and

Israel is in a permanent state of crisis. In other words, during the "Hebrew period" tribalism is strong and monotheism is weak. The full impact of the universality and supremacy of God is not yet established among the Hebrews. Someone must take it to the next level.

That someone is Jeremiah.

Jeremiah begins the process that will result in the transition from Hebrew to Jew, or from tribalism and incipient monotheism to a permanent monotheistic culture practiced by the Jew both individually and communally. Jeremiah is the first person of his time to grasp that while pagan gods disappear when the people who worship them are conquered and destroyed, the God of the universe never disappears, and since this God made a covenant with the people of Israel, this people will endure. In the final analysis, the existence of this people does not depend on political sovereignty. Sovereignty may be gained or lost, but the covenant between God and Israel is forever. "Not by might nor by power but by my spirit says Adonai of Hosts," a later prophet will proclaim after the return of the exiles from Babylonia, echoing Jeremiah's teaching (Zechariah 4:6). Might and power are only valid when exerted in keeping with the spirit of God's will. This is the lesson Jeremiah's contemporaries had failed to learn, but those who later return from exile do learn thanks to him. Here is where the transformation from Hebrew to Jew takes place.[7]

It is important to point out that after the time of Jeremiah pagan practices all but disappear from Jewish life. Stories to this effect appear in biblical books dating to the time of the Babylonian and post-Babylonian exile. One example is the Book of Esther, where Mordecai is portrayed as a proud Jew who refuses to assimilate into Persian culture. Another is the Book of Daniel, where the young exile from Jerusalem refuses to assimilate into Babylonian culture. From now on, adhering to the faith of Israel and rejecting paganism becomes for the Jew an article of faith, best exemplified in the Maccabean revolt against Greek paganism during the time of the Second Temple.

9.

Making Torah a Reality

After the scroll of the Torah was found in the Temple, King Josiah launched a major reform and, having cleansed his realm of all manner of idolatry, he assembled all the people in Jerusalem and had the scroll read to the multitude, whereupon the covenant between God and Israel was renewed. What Jeremiah makes clear is that despite this great show of public religious reaffirmation, the precepts of the Torah did not make a lasting impression on the listeners. As soon as the ensuing public celebration of Passover was over, people returned to their pagan practices and to their immoral ways. Jeremiah proceeds to chastise the court's priests and prophets, literally "those who hold the Torah" (*tofsey ha'torah*), for failing to discharge their duty, namely, teach the Torah in such a way that it becomes a living reality.

This task is left to Jeremiah himself, who will be spending his long prophetic career weaving the precepts of the book of Deuteronomy—which contains the essence of the entire Torah—through all his pronouncements, whereby for the first time in the history of his people the Torah is not only the lofty blueprint of an ideal society followed by a small elite, but the living source of faith and ethical living for all the people.

A remarkable example of this method of teaching is the way in which Jeremiah interprets the Ten Commandments and applies them to the lives of his contemporaries. The Ten Commandments are known in Hebrew as the Ten Spoken Statements (*aseret ha'dibrot*). When the Torah is given at Mount Sinai, we are told that God speaks to the children of Israel and pronounces the Ten Commandments, beginning with "I am Adonai your God." Moses is then given two stone tablets upon which the Ten Commandments are engraved "by the finger of God" (Exodus 31:19). Thus, the Ten Commandments are the only part of the law spoken by God and heard by the entire people (the only time this ever happens), and the only one handed down in writing. The tablets upon which the commandments are written are called the Tablets of the Covenant, whereby the observance of these ten statements represents the compliance with the covenant.

Jeremiah weaves the Ten Commandments in his prophetic messages, starting with his early prophecies, when the young Jeremiah makes an impassioned plea about the oneness of God and the exodus from Egypt, echoing the first commandment, "I am Adonai your God who took you out of the land of Egypt" (Deut. 5:6). As for the second commandment, "You shall not have other gods besides Me," this will be his lifelong message, indeed, the centerpiece of his prophetic teachings. The third commandment, "You shall not swear falsely by the name of Adonai your God," is echoed in his admonitions against the priests and the prophets who pay lip service to their task of teaching the Torah to the people, and thereby compromise themselves.

The fourth commandment, "Remember the Sabbath day and keep it holy," appears in an episode in which God commands Jeremiah to speak to the people who enter Jerusalem through its various gates, and admonish them regarding carrying merchandise or produce into the city on the Sabbath, or doing any manner of work on that day:

> Thus said Adonai: Guard yourselves for your own
> sake against carrying burdens on the Sabbath day,
> and bringing these through the gates of Jerusalem.
> Nor shall you carry out burdens from your houses
> on the Sabbath day, as I commanded your ancestors. . . .
> If you obey me, declares Adonai, and do not bring in
> burdens through the gates of this city on the Sabbath
> day, but hallow the Sabbath day and do not work
> on it, then through the gates of this city shall enter
> kings who will sit upon the throne of David. . . ." (17:21-25)

Here Jeremiah extols the observance of the Sabbath as central to the survival and welfare of Judaism, which indeed has been the case throughout post-biblical history (in the famous words of the modern Hebrew philosopher Ahad Ha'am, "More than the Jews kept the Sabbath, the Sabbath kept the Jews"). It is clear from this episode that at the end of the monarchic period the observance of the Sabbath was lax, and the prohibition of working on the Sabbath was loosely interpreted by the farmers and the merchants, who brought their goods to Jerusalem from the countryside on the Sabbath. The priests and the official prophets of the day looked the other way, and it was left to Jeremiah to remind the people that the prohibition of work on the Sabbath is absolute.

It should be pointed out that the centrality of the Sabbath as the sign of the covenant between God and Israel becomes well established after the time of Jeremiah, when the exiles begin to return to Jerusalem from Babylonia. It seems to this writer that this episode in the book of Jeremiah plays a major part in this. The question, however, has been raised as to whether the episode is authentic, or was added later on. In the overall context of the book, there is no doubt that Jeremiah put great emphasis on the observance of the Sabbath, and most likely did show up at the gates of Jerusalem to chastise the people for violating the

Sabbath, whether or not this story was later rewritten in the spirit of post-exilic religion.

The fifth commandment refers to honoring one's parents. Here the story of the Rechabites (35:1-19) comes to mind. During Nebuchadnezzar's siege on Jerusalem, a tribe known as Rechabites seeks shelter in the besieged city. Its members are known to lead an ascetic life. Jeremiah invites them to the Temple and offers them wine. They respond by saying that their ancestor had forbidden them to drink wine. Jeremiah upholds their filial loyalty as an example of obedience and respect for parents, contrasting it with the people's lack of respect for God's commandments.

This commandment is followed by the five "you shall not" commandments. The first four—murder, adultery, theft and lying appear in a statement made by Jeremiah while he addresses people entering the newly refurbished Temple in Jerusalem. It is clear to Jeremiah that the throng entering the renovated Temple includes more than a few people who are guilty of one or more of those transgressions, yet they all seem to feel that by coming to the Temple and making an offering all their sins are forgiven. Jeremiah mocks them by saying:

> Do not trust in this false reassurance, saying,
> Adonai's Temple, Adonai's Temple,
> Adonai's Temple it is.   (7:4)

No, the Temple and the sacrificial offerings do not automatically grant forgiveness. One must first change one's ways and pursue righteousness. He goes on to say:

> Will you steal, and commit murder,
> and commit adultery,
> and swear falsely,
> and burn incense to the Baal,
> and pursue other gods whom you know not?
> And then you would come and stand before
> this house that bears My name and you say,
> We were saved so that we can commit all these
> abominations.   (7:9-10)

It is interesting to note that in this capsule recital of the Decalogue Jeremiah reverses the order of the commandments and puts the ones dealing with the sins against other people before the one dealing with the sins against God. Was he implying that immorality was more serious than idolatry? Was immorality more prevalent at that time? Clearly, there is an important message in this passage.

The last commandment reads:

> You shall not covet your neighbor's house;
> You shall not covet your neighbor's wife,
> Or his male or female slave,
> Or his ox or his ass,
> Or anything that is your neighbor's.
> (Deuteronomy 5:17)

This commandment is reflected in the following statement Jeremiah makes regarding the young men of Jerusalem:

> They are like well-fed horses
> who neigh at their neighbor's wife. (5:8)

Jeremiah, who is known to us primarily as the prophet who predicts the destruction of Jerusalem and the return from Babylonian exile seventy years later, is in reality first and foremost the teacher of the Torah, who lays the groundwork for the Torah to become for all the generations that follow him the book they live by. Everything he sees around him is given, so to speak, the Torah test. If it deviates in the slightest way from the standards set by the Torah, he exposes it and decries it. One small act of injustice by one member of the community is a virus threatening the spiritual health of the entire community. It must be exposed and denounced. It is incumbent upon the entire community to see to it that the weak members of society—the stranger, the orphan, the widow—are not oppressed or wronged. It is also incumbent upon the entire community not to tolerate idolatry. The Torah teaches individual as well as communal responsibility. A society is only as good as the sum total of its members. A few bad members, and particularly a few bad leaders, can bring great harm upon the entire society.

These are but a few examples of the many Torah lessons embedded in the prophecies of Jeremiah which cover a period of some forty years, yet are not always readily apparent,. These lessons were preserved when the prophecies were collected and written down by Jeremiah's scribe Baruch ben Neriah and then copied shortly after the prophet's death, most likely first in Egypt, where he was exiled along with his scribe, and then in Babylonia, which became the new center of Jewish life, and were carefully studied by the exiles who would return to Jerusalem seventy years after the destruction and begin to introduce the precepts of the prophets to their daily lives.

10.

Do Not Pray for These People

Early in the book, God tells Jeremiah:

> Do not pray for these people and do not raise your voice in song
> and prayer for them. And do not plead with me, for I am not
> listening to you. (7:16)

An explanation follows:

> Can't you see what they are doing in the towns of Judah
> and in the streets of Jerusalem?
> The sons gather wood, and the fathers kindle the fire,
> and the women knead dough to make cakes for the
> Queen of Heaven, and to pour out drink-offerings for
> other gods to annoy Me. (7:17-18)

Clearly, the so-called Queen of Heaven was a popular pagan deity among the Judeans, and so were other deities. The people carried a heavy burden of disobedience to God that dated back to the time of the Exodus and stretched over centuries, during which time God had sent "the prophets My servants day and night" (7:25) but to no avail. Therefore, "Do not pray for these people." It is too late to repent.

Slowly, the realization begins to sink in. Judah is doomed. Only destruction and exile will bring redemption. Jeremiah is devastated. He begins to have nightmares. Every night he sees visions of the coming catastrophe. He can hear the thunder of a thousand galloping horses rolling down from the north and the shouts of horsemen; he can see the flashes of swords and spears; he hears the cries of the first victims who are cut down in the fields as the enemy heads for the fortified cities. He sees the slaughter in Jerusalem, where no family is spared. He wakes up in a cold sweat, and he begins to mourn those who will soon die:

> Would that my head turned to water,
> And my eyes to a fountain of tears,
> That I may weep day and night
> For the slain of the daughter of my people! (8:23)

At this point we are witnessing a prophetic paradox. While the prophet knows that destruction is imminent, he does not give up his mission. His mission is not for the here and now, but rather for the ages. And yet, he does not give up completely on his contemporaries. Where there is life there is hope. Jeremiah is not simply a soldier who takes orders from his commander. He has a mind of his own, and he believes that God may reconsider. In so doing he reminds us of Abraham, who pleads with God on behalf of the wicked city of Sodom, and of Moses, who intercedes with God to save his people after they erect the golden calf. Even in the worst of situations there is always a glimmer of hope.

Moreover, Jeremiah is convinced that although God had told him not to pray for these people, God still expects him to look for ways to impress upon them how they had failed God. It then occurs to him that he needs to do more than talk, admonish, plead and cry. He needs to dramatize the prophetic message and use something tangible to drive it home, the way God used the blossoming almond branch and the boiling pot as a vehicle to induct the young Jeremiah into the prophetic vocation.

God tells Jeremiah:

> Go buy yourself a loincloth of linen, and put it around your loins, but do not dip it in water. So I bought the loincloth as ordered by God and I wore it. And God spoke to me again saying, Take the loincloth you bought and are now wearing and go to Perath and put it in a cleft in the rock. So I went and hid it in Perath as God had commanded me. Much later, God said to me, Go to Perath and retrieve the loincloth I had commanded you to hide there. So I went to Perath and I dug up the loincloth from the place where I had buried it, and found the loincloth ruined and useless. (13:1-7)

Jeremiah does not tell us how exactly he presents the soggy, torn loincloth to his listeners. Most likely, he wears it under his robe, and when he tells the story of the loincloth to a crowd in Jerusalem, they wonder where that undergarment is. He loosens his belt and much to the crowd's surprise they see the loincloth wrapped around his hips, dirty and wet. He goes on to explain that just as this cloth was destroyed and was of no use, so will the people of Judah and Jerusalem be destroyed for their arrogance in abandoning God's commands. Furthermore, Jeremiah explains, just as this wet cloth clings to my loins, so did God make all of Israel and all of Judah cling to Him as His own glorious people, but they did not heed the word of God and the cloth was destroyed.

What kind of impression did this story make on the prophet's listeners? Certainly it did not endear him to them. We can only deduce from the fact that it did not lead to any real consequences that most people shook their heads at this strange behavior and shrugged it off. The Bible on several occasions tells us that there is a thin line between a prophet and a madman, and quite often people during the prophetic age had to wonder whether a particular action by a prophet was a sign from God or a sign of mental derangement. One may conclude in this particular instance Jeremiah was so desperate to make his point that he was acting in a way that most people would have taken to be less than judicious.

11.

Mother Dear, Why Was I Born?

We can see Jeremiah on a late summer evening in Jerusalem. He is lying on his bed with a candle burning in the corner. He watches the shadows dance on the ceiling, and he thinks of the spectacle he had made of himself earlier that day with that dirty, soggy loincloth. Not only did the crowd refuse to take him seriously, some had shouted epithets at him and even called him *meshuggah*, crazy. Perhaps they were right. Was it God's will for him to do such a strange thing in front of the crowd? For what purpose? Wasn't he wasting his time and making a fool of himself?

He hears a knock on the door. He is too tired to get up. Someone calls his name. It's a familiar voice.

Jeremiah, my son, open up!

He now recognizes his mother's voice. He hasn't seen his mother in a long time. His father had recently passed away, and his old mother went back to live with her family in Anathoth.

Jeremiah gets up, wraps himself in his robe, and opens the door. His mother's silvery hair shines in the dark. She puts her arms around him and holds him for a long time.

He offers her the only chair in the room and brings her a jar of water.

I was thinking of you a great deal lately, mother dear, he says, and I was going to go to Anathoth to visit you, but here you are.

It is a good thing you didn't go, my son.

Why?

You won't be safe there.

Why not?

Some of the priests there are saying you have become the enemy of the people. Instead of reassuring them God is on their side, you keep telling them they are doomed. They think it would be best to get rid of you.

They remain silent for a long time.

Be careful, my son, his mother cautions.

Jeremiah thinks of his beloved Anathoth. Why did he give up such a beautiful place where his roots ran so deep for the hustle and bustle of this city that brought him nothing but heartache? He feels he has reached the bottom of the abyss. He looks at his mother with eyes brimming with pain,

Mother, oh mother dear, why was I born? I quarrel with the whole world, and I know nothing but strife. But why? I have never lent or borrowed money, yet everyone curses me.

Why don't you reconcile yourself to your uncles the priests, and return to the fold? His mother pleads. You can catch more flies with honey than with vinegar.

I should, shouldn't I? There is no point to what I am doing. I am wasting my time. I do things I don't want to do. I know there is something wrong with me.

You were such a happy boy, his mother says with a sad smile. You were such a good student. By now you could have succeeded your father as high priest. You could have been second to the king. And here you are, in mid-life, without a wife, all alone. Come back, my son, come back.

Jeremiah breaks into tears.

I can't help myself, he cries. It's like fire burning in my bones. Why me, God, why me?

12.

Speaking Truth to Power

The fire continued to burn in Jeremiah's bones, but Jeremiah, like the burning bush, was not consumed. No matter what happened to him, no matter what anyone did or said, the word of God could not be stopped. No one has ever put it better than the prophet Amos: "When a lion roars, who is not afraid? When God speaks, who will not prophesy?" (2:8). Prophecy in ancient Israel was not a matter of choice. It was an absolute, life-long commitment. No prophet ever ceased to be a prophet. Whether one was a shepherd like Moses, or a farmer like Amos, or a priest like Jeremiah, once the prophetic call was heard, there was no turning back. That person has now become the conduit of God's word and would remain one to the end.

One thing all the Hebrew prophets understood during the entire period of the monarchy: the kingdom of Israel was a small nation surrounded by much stronger powers. The true strength of Israel was not military, but rather moral and spiritual. The king and his advisors, on the other hand, often lost sight of this reality. They would get caught up in the game of regional power politics, and more often than not would bring great harm to their people.

During the reign of King Josiah, the last righteous king, Jeremiah had no quarrel with the king, who had done all he could to restore Israel's covenantal relationship with their God, and put his energy into social and religious reform instead of regional politics. Instead, Jeremiah went directly to the people and for several years delivered his prophetic message in places of public gathering. After the death of King Josiah, however, it became clear to the prophet that Judah could no longer ignore the new political reality in the region and continue to function as an independent state. It was time to bring this message directly to the ruling class, and particularly to the king.

Jeremiah first reaches this conclusion during the reign of Jehoahaz, Josiah's son and successor, who reigned for all of three months. The twenty-three-year-old king was the choice of the people, but the people failed to take one thing into account—their dead king had defied the Pharaoh and was defeated, and the Pharaoh now considered Judah his realm. No sooner was Jehoahaz crowned than emissaries from Pharaoh Necho II showed up in Jerusalem and informed the court they expected the courtesy of approving the new king. Furthermore, they expected the vanquished kingdom to pay a monetary tribute to the Pharaoh. There was no one to turn to for help, so the court capitulated. The Pharaoh ordered Jehoahaz to be exiled to Egypt, and in his place he crowned his brother, Eliakim, and changed his name to Jehoiakim to let the people of Judah know who it was that named their king.

Jeremiah understood this was not just a temporary setback. The days of the kingdom were numbered. It was God's will, and it was the result of years of moral decline. The people, on the other hand, hoped that their beloved young king would return from Egypt, but Jeremiah knew he would never come back. He begins his campaign against false political expectations, which he knows can only lead to disaster. From now on, in addition to being Israel's voice of conscience, he takes on the role of a political activist. Letting the court know the exiled king will not come back, he says:

> Weep not for the dead, do not bemoan him,
> But weep bitterly for him who goes away,
> For he shall not return, nor see his native land.
> For thus says Adonai regarding Shallum [Jehoahaz]
> son of Josiah, King of Judah, who reigned instead of
> Josiah his father, and who went forth from this place:
> He shall never return. For he shall die in the place
> where he has been exiled, and shall not see this land
> any more. (22:10-12)

Needless to say, Jeremiah does not make any friends or wins the hearts of too many people with this bitter prediction. And as best we can tell, the new king, Jehoahaz's brother Jehoiakim, does not take him to task over this statement, for he seems to be quite satisfied to be the new king. What Jeremiah will soon find out, however, is that his own troubles are about to begin in earnest.

Jehoiakim does not start his career as a popular king. This is due to two reasons: First, he is saddled with the task of collecting the tribute for the Pharaoh, and second, to make matters worse, he goes about doing it mercilessly, without any regard as to who can afford what. In the process, he robs the poor and orders his tax collectors to arrest, torture, and even put to death those who cannot meet his quota. He also takes advantage of the tribute collection to raise money for a new palace for himself. Jeremiah, as can be expected, does not stand by quietly. He returns to the Temple square and speaks out against the king:

> Woe to him who builds his house without righteousness,
> And his chambers without justice;
> Who uses his neighbor's services without wages,
> And withholds his pay.
> Who says: I will build myself a spacious house
> With large chambers, and fashion myself windows,
> And use varnished cedar panels.

Will you reign because you excel in cedar?
Did not your father eat and drink and yet did justice
And righteousness? Then it was well with him.
He judged the cause of the poor and the needy,
Then it was well. Is not this to know Me? says Adonai.
But your eyes and your heart are only set on
Your covetousness, and on shedding innocent blood,
And on oppression, and violence, to do it.
Therefore thus says Adonai concerning Jehoiakim son of
Josiah, King of Judah: They shall not lament him:
'Ah my brother,' or "Ah sister!
They shall lament him: 'Ah Lord, or "Ah, his glory.'
He shall be buried the burial of an ass,
Drawn and cast forth beyond the gates of
Jerusalem. (22:13-19)

Jeremiah has begun to put his life at risk. Jehoiakim was a ruthless monarch who would not think twice about putting Jeremiah to death. How he gets away with such a blunt prophecy is hard to explain. And what is particularly hard to understand is how he gets away with such a graphic description of the ignominious end the king was to encounter. Moreover, one wonders whether God provides the prophet with a crystal ball that allows him to glimpse the future with such precise detail, or whether he is making an educated guess. Knowing the history of the kings of Judah and Israel, it is not difficult for Jeremiah to envision this kind of an end for the evil king. Nevertheless, the prophet delivers his message in the name of God, and this is how he expects us to understand it.

13.

Jeremiah Faces Death

Jeremiah was not without followers. They were few in number, but some of them were close to the royal family, and that would soon prove to be quite critical for his welfare, as we shall find out. One of those people was a man a few years younger than him, named Baruch ben Neriah. When Jeremiah first leaves home and goes to live in Jerusalem where he supports himself teaching the laws of the Torah, Baruch becomes one of his first students, and will remain close to him to the very end. Their relationship is one of master and disciple. Baruch was as devoted to Jeremiah as Joshua was to Moses or Elisha to Elijah. People wondered whether Jeremiah might pass the mantle of prophecy to his disciple when the time came, and Baruch himself often thought about it, waking up in the middle of the night from a dream in which he thought he heard the voice of God. But it was not meant to be. Baruch's mission was to record and preserve the words of Jeremiah for future generations. Jeremiah already had a successor he was not aware of, a young boy named Ezekiel who, in a few years, would be sent to Babylonia with the first deportation, where he would continue Jeremiah's mission among the Judean exiles.

After Jehoiakim became king, Baruch began to fear for Jeremiah's life. His contacts at the king's court told him that the king was outraged by Jeremiah's prophecy regarding the king's greed and excesses resulting in such a humiliating death. Everything you say may be true, Baruch argued, but this king is not Josiah. He is capable of anything.

As if uttering a prophecy, something happened soon after that proved Baruch right. It appears that Jeremiah was not the only one who was predicting the coming destruction of the Temple and of Jerusalem. Another prophet by the name of Uriah son of Shemaiah of Kiriath Yearim appeared before the king and the princes and all the mighty men, and told them they were bringing destruction upon themselves and their people. The king ordered his men to seize Uriah and put him to death, but Uriah managed to escape and fled to Egypt. The king sent emissaries to Egypt and brought the prophet back to Jerusalem, where the king himself slew him with his sword and had his body thrown into a common grave (26:20-23).

It was time for Jeremiah to lay low, but he refused to do so. Now more than ever before it is time for me to speak out, he told Baruch, who kept begging him to change his mind. God has assured me that nothing would happen to me, Jeremiah insisted. God said to me:

> Gird up your loins and rise and tell them
> All that I command you; do not buckle before them

Lest I break you down before them.
I turn you this day into a fortified city
And an iron pillar, and bronze walls
Against the whole land—
Against Judah's kings and counselors
And against its priests and citizens.
They will fight you but they will not defeat you,
For I am with you, declares Adonai, to save you.
(1:17-19)

You see, Baruch, Jeremiah told his disciple, the only one I have to fear is God.

Baruch relented. He knew he could argue with his master, but he could not argue with God.

The next day the word of God came to Jeremiah, This time the divine command was unequivocal:

Stand in the court of God's House
and tell those of the cities of Judah
who come to worship in God's House,
all the words which I command
you to speak to them,
do not omit a word. (26:2)

And here we have another divine paradox. God has already given up on these people, yet God, like Jeremiah, is hoping against hope they may listen to the prophet and repent.

Jeremiah does exactly as he is told. It is late summer, and there is a large crowd in the Temple's courtyard. He climbs the stairs and faces the crowd and delivers his message. He reminds the crowd of all the prophets God has sent them over and over again, but to no avail. God wants them to know that if they do not change their ways this Temple will be destroyed like the temple at Shiloh, where the Ark of the Covenant and the divine presence dwelled before they were moved to Jerusalem.

That the Temple may be destroyed is the last thing the crowd wants to hear. Several court priests and prophets turn to the crowd and tell the people to seize Jeremiah and put him on trial for his life. Unlike Uriah, Jeremiah does not try to escape. He lets his captors take him to the new gate of the House of God, where a court is quickly assembled, with the crowd pressing in from all sides. Word is sent to the king's palace across the way, and before long the king's officials show up and join the priests and the prophets who have now formed a tribunal seeking the death sentence for Jeremiah.

The most senior of the priests turns to Jeremiah and says,

Do you, Jeremiah son of Hilkiah admit that you said that this House of God will become like the one in Shiloh, and that this city will be destroyed and left without inhabitants?

Yes, I did.

The priest turns to the king's officials and says,

This man admits he has said the things you have just heard. This man must die.

Jeremiah turns to the crowd and to the king's officials.

God has sent me to prophesy concerning this House and this city, he says in a weary voice. God has told me all these things. Change your ways and your acts, and listen to Adonai your God, and Adonai will renounce the punishment he has decreed for you. As for me, I am in your hands. Do with me as you please. But know this, if you kill me you will have innocent blood on your hands and on this city and on all its inhabitants, for truly God has sent me to speak to you and tell you all these things (26:12-15).

The priest turns to the highest-ranking official of the king's court and asks him for his opinion. Ultimately, this matter has to be turned over to the king, whom this official represents. The priest has no doubt in his mind the official would agree with the recommendation of the court. Much to his surprise, the official replies,

We cannot sentence this man to death, for he speaks in the name of Adonai our God.

Stunned, the priest turns to the crowd.

What say you?

You can't kill him, someone shouts out, for he speaks in the name of Adonai our God.

The crowd seems to be in agreement, although people start to debate the issue with one another.

The presiding priest silences the crowd.

Let us hear from our elders, he says.

In ancient Israel, while the prophets received the word of God and the priests had to implement it, the elders were the voice of common wisdom, as we learn from such biblical books as the book of Proverbs and the book of Ecclesiastes, which form part of the Bible's wisdom literature.

One elder, whose looks remind people of Moses, steps forward and says,

There was a prophet named Micah, the Morashtite, who prophesied in the days of King Hezekiah of Judah, and he said to all the people of Judah, Thus said the God of Hosts, Zion shall be plowed as a field, Jerusalem shall become heaps of ruins, and the Temple Mount a high place in the woods. Did King Hezekiah of Judah, and all of Judah, put him to death? No, the king feared Adonai and Adonai renounced the punishment He had decreed against them. Beware, we are about to do great harm to ourselves.

The elder bows his head to the tribunal and steps back into the crowd. No one speaks. All those who have been clamoring for Jeremiah's head seem to be having a change of heart. It appears that contrary to the case of Uriah, whom the king undoubtedly was able to discredit and proclaim a false prophet whom the king was free to kill, when Jeremiah spoke in his own defense and made it clear he was not afraid to die since it was not him but God who was speaking, the king's official, whose name we are told was Ahikam son of Shaphan, could sense that Jeremiah spoke the truth, and could further sense that the people also realized they were hearing the word of God. In the Second Book of Kings we are told that when King Josiah asked Jeremiah's father, the high priest Hilkiah, to find a prophet who can explain the message of the scroll Hilkiah found in the Temple, he also asks Ahikam the son of Shaphan to go along. Clearly, Ahikam, who was about Jeremiah's age, knew Jeremiah well and knew him to be a true prophet, although, as a member of the king's entourage, he was not always free to speak his mind. This time, however, he decided to save Jeremiah's life, feeling certain that public opinion was on his side (26:24).

When King Jehoiakim heard about the Temple trial he was furious. But there was nothing he could do about it. He could not publicly defy Jeremiah. He would have to think of a surreptitious way to get rid of this troublemaker.

14.

Write Down These Words

Jeremiah returns to his home accompanied by Baruch. The two of them sit down without speaking a word. Jeremiah's hands begin to shake. His head drops and he covers his face with his hands. He now realizes that while he was facing his accusers God made him fearless; but now, in the privacy of his home, the thought of how close he came to dying makes him tremble with fear. Ahikam has put his own life on the line for him, but what would the king have to say? Baruch was right. He was no longer safe. He had a mission to fulfill, but dead prophets cannot fulfill any missions.

Baruch did not say anything to his master. He knew that Jeremiah would go back to the Temple in a heartbeat and do exactly what he had just done. The prophet had to be protected from himself. And so Baruch went the next day to see Ahikam at the king's court and told him to issue an order forbidding Jeremiah from going back to the Temple. Ahikam was happy to comply. He too was concerned about what might happen to Jeremiah if he went back.

A year goes by without any prophetic activity on the part of Jeremiah. That year, 605 BCE, Pharaoh's army travels north again to join Assyria in her decisive battle against the Babylonians, led by Nebuchadnezzar, the son and heir of the Babylonian king Nabopolassar. The Babylonians win a decisive victory at Carchemish, on the northern banks of the Euphrates, and the Assyrian Empire ceases to exist. Egypt loses its military might and becomes a second-rate power, no longer capable of exerting regional influence. From now on, the Babylonian Empire under Nebuchadnezzar becomes the dominant power in the entire region, and will remain in control for the next sixty-five years, until its defeat at the hands of King Cyrus the Great of Persia.

At first, King Jehoiakim is jubilant. He no longer has to pay tribute to the Egyptians. Jeremiah, on the other hand, is apprehensive. He now realizes that when he first heard God's call, he was shown a sign of how "trouble will come from the north," and now that Egypt was defeated, this trouble was sure to come. We know from ancient Babylonian records that the following year, 604, Nebuchadnezzar launched his first campaign down the coast of Judah, where he captured and ransacked the coastal city of Ashkelon. The king of Judah now understood he was about to have his old master replaced by a new one.

Once again, as happened to him during the time of King Josiah, Jeremiah is beset by nightmares about the onslaught from the north. Now the enemy has a name, and it is clear to him that the little kingdom of Judah is no match for such a formidable foe. It now occurs to him that the most important thing to preserve for the future is the words and the laws that support the covenant, namely, the Torah. The book of the Torah that was found in the Temple in the days of Josiah was only a partial record of Deuteronomy. There were other oral traditions, dating back to Moses, which had to be incorporated into the text. With the imminent destruction of Jerusalem, the oral traditions were doomed to disappear. And then there was the historical record of the time of Moses, the stories of Joshua, the Judges, Samuel, and the time of the monarchy, beginning with Saul, David and Solomon, and continuing with the kings of the divided monarchy up to the present. All of this had to be assembled, edited, and written down in a final version and preserved for future generations.

Thus begins what will become perhaps the most important literary collaboration in history. Jeremiah enlists the help of his able disciple, Baruch son of Neriah, perhaps the most level-headed and methodical thinker and writer of his generation, and together they begin to assemble and write down the final versions of the books of Deuteronomy, Joshua, Judges, First and Second Samuel, and First and Second Kings (Baruch will complete the latter during his exile in Egypt after the fall of Jerusalem), which will later be sent for safekeeping to the exiles in Babylonia, from where Ezra will bring them back to Jerusalem when King Cyrus of Persia orders the rebuilding of the "Temple in Jerusalem in the land of Judah" (Ezra 1:2).[8]

Jeremiah knows he has to alert the people and the king about the great danger facing Judah. He also knows he must do something to preserve his own prophecies in case anything happens to him. It is then that God tells him to write down all his prophecies, from the time of Josiah to the present:

> Take a scroll and write down all the words that
> I have spoken to you concerning Israel and Judah
> and all the nations, from the day I first spoke
> to you in the days of Josiah to this day. (36:2)

Jeremiah charges Baruch with this task, and Baruch is happy to comply. He now becomes Jeremiah's scribe, and it will become his life's mission to record and preserve his master's words. He writes down all the prophecies with ink on parchment, creating the first version of the scroll or the book of Jeremiah. The prophet tells his disciple to take the scroll to the Temple, "since I am detained and cannot go to the Temple" (36:5), and read it to the people on a public fast day. He tells him he hopes that by reading the scroll to them, each one of them will repent and return to God (as happened when the scroll was found in the Temple and prompted young King Josiah to repent).

It is the ninth month of the fifth year of the reign of King Jehoiakim, corresponding to December 604 BCE, a rather cold snowy day in Jerusalem, when the people gather for a public fast, probably in an attempt to find favor with the God of their fathers who might listen to their prayers and perform the same miracle He once performed during the time of King Hezekiah, Josiah's great-grandfather, when King Sennacherib of Assyria came to lay siege to Jerusalem and his army was miraculously slaughtered during the night. Everyone knows such miracles do not occur too often, and no one is too hopeful. But the first question is: Will Nebuchadnezzar's army show up and demand tribute or, worse yet, lay siege to Jerusalem?

Baruch knows he is risking his life by bringing his master's message to the people at a time like this. But this does not stop him from carrying out the mission. He wraps himself in a winter coat made of sheepskin, and walks up to the Temple courtyard. The guard recognizes him and directs him to the chamber of Gemariah son of Shaphan the scribe, the man in charge of records, whose father was one of the people King Josiah had sent to find a prophet who could interpret the message of the scroll found in the Temple (II Kings 22:12).[9]

How is Jeremiah doing? Gemariah inquires, we haven't seen him in a long time.

He is well, Baruch replies. You know he is forbidden from entering the Temple grounds.

Oh, yes, I forgot, Gemariah chuckles. He almost had himself put to death last time he was here. Tell me, Baruch, you know this man almost better than anyone else, except perhaps for his own mother. What kind of man is he? What is he like with you, in the privacy of his home? Is he different from the public man who is always trying to put the fear of God into us?

Baruch hesitates. Is he at liberty to talk about his master's private life? Gemariah, however, is a friend. He is genuinely interested in finding out what Jeremiah is like.

He is my master, Baruch replies. He is almost old enough to be my father. But most of the time I feel he is the child and I am the adult. There is an innocence about him that is hard to explain. He has to be protected from himself. One moment he can be joyous or even ecstatic, and the next moment he falls into the abyss of despair. It is not so easy to keep up with him, but I wouldn't give him up for anything in the world.

Do you think you may become his successor?

No, I don't think so. I must admit when I was young I entertained such thoughts. But I have learned from living with him that it takes a special kind of person to be a prophet. You have to be able to completely open yourself up and let God into your soul. You have to think with your heart, not your mind. That is not me.

So what brings you here?

He has sent me here with this scroll of his prophecies and he would like me to read it to the people.

Gemariah puts his hand on Baruch's shoulder.

Are you up to the task? Remember what happened last time Jeremiah came and prophesied here.

I put myself in God's hands, Baruch replies.

Well, then, let us go to the upper court by the new gate and you will read it to the people.

On the way to the gate Gemariah turns to Baruch and pulls him back by the arm. The two stop. Gemariah says,

No one wants to hear what Jeremiah has to say, because no one wants to hear the truth. I remember him saying some years ago, "Trouble will come from the north," and here we are, no longer under Egyptian yoke, but now we are waiting for the new enemy from the north, who has already come down with his mighty army, ready to show up in Jerusalem. All the other so-called prophets have lied to us, telling us things we wanted to hear. Only Jeremiah spoke the truth. God be with you, Baruch, for you are bringing the word of our God to our people.

It is too cold outside, and since the people are fasting they need shelter from the cold. Gemariah calls them back into the chamber where he directs Baruch to read the scroll to the people.

The people are looking for reassurance. They want to know that God is on their side. But they are told that they have angered their God, and unless they change their ways they will face destruction and exile. Some of them might have heard some of those prophecies before, but they had paid little attention. Now that they are fasting and their spirits are contrite, it is to be expected that they would be more receptive to what Jeremiah has to say. When Baruch finishes reading the scroll, however, there is dead silence. No one speaks. Gemariah realizes that, once again, Jeremiah's words have fallen on deaf ears. He leaves the chamber and tells his son, Micaiah, to keep an eye on things until he gets back.

It appears that Jeremiah's words made a deep impression on Micaiah. He decides to report what he has just heard to the king's scribe, Elishama, at the king's palace. When Micaiah arrives at the scribe's chamber, he finds several of the king's counselors sitting around the table with Elishama the scribe. He tells Elishama he has just heard some dire prophecies attributed to Jeremiah, which he felt should be made known to the king's court. One of the officials says,

I remember a year ago Jeremiah was at the Temple and his words infuriated the people. He came within a hair's breadth of his life. Let us bring Baruch over and let him read us this scroll.

We should consult the rest of the counselors before we bring him here, some-one suggests.

They all agree, and they summon the rest of the king's officials, who decide to bring Baruch over.

It is only a short distance from the Temple to the king's palace, and Baruch soon shows up.

Baruch walks slowly into Elishama's chamber, and the assembled officials can tell he is afraid.

Please sit down, make yourself at home, someone says reassuringly. We would like you to read the scroll to us.

Once again, Baruch recites Jeremiah's words. When he is done, the king's officials look at one another, and this time they are the ones who look apprehensive.

What shall we tell the king? One of them says.

At this point one may wonder: Why don't they simply dismiss Jeremiah's words as they have done so many times in the past? Why do they feel they have to bring them to the king's attention?

One possible explanation is that until now they have only heard Jeremiah speak and they chose to ignore him. This time, for the first time, they are faced with a written scroll. A written document carries much more weight than the spoken word. Words can be forgotten, but a written text has a life of its own. And especially now, during a time of national emergency and in the midst of a public fast, the written prophecy seems inescapable.

Did he dictate those words to you? they ask Baruch. They want to be sure Baruch did not write them from memory, or added anything of his own, but was rather delivering the exact words of the prophet.

Yes, says Baruch, he spoke, and as he spoke I wrote down the words with ink on this scroll (36:18).

They decide they have to bring the matter to the attention of the king.

You and your master better go into hiding, they tell Baruch. Let no one know where you are. There is no telling what the king might do to you.

Clearly, they talk to Baruch like a member of their ruling class, and are being frank about the king's disposition. They would not talk like this to a commoner.

They take the scroll and give it to Elishama for safekeeping, and they send a messenger to inform the king about it. The king asks for the scroll to be brought to him. Jehudi, the king's servant, goes and fetches the scroll and brings it to the king, who is sitting in the winter wing of his palace, in front of the blazing fire.

Jehudi starts to read, and when he reaches the fourth sheet of the scroll (the scroll is made of sheets of parchment sewn together), the king, speaking in an angry voice, tells him to stop reading and waves at him to hand over the scroll. Yehudi bows his head and holds out the scroll. The king snatches the scroll from his hand. The king is holding a shaving razor in his other hand. He walks over to the fireplace. Elnathan, Delaiah and Gemariah implore the king not to burn the scroll, but he ignores them. He takes the scroll and slashes it into pieces, feeding the pieces to the fire until the last piece turns to ashes.

Here the biblical writer (most likely Baruch) adds an editorial comment:

> And the king and his servants who had heard all
> those things did not fear and did not tear their
> garments. (36:24)

The allusion is clear. Unlike King Josiah and his men, who tore their garments and were overcome with fear after hearing the Temple scroll read to them, this king was irredeemable and his servants were too afraid to disagree with him. Clearly, the public fast was a sham. The fear of God was nowhere to be found.

The story concludes:

> The king ordered Jerahmeel, the king's son,
> and Seraiah son of Azriel, and Shelemiah son
> of Abdiel to arrest Baruch the scribe and
> Jeremiah the prophet. But Adonai hid them.
> (36:26)

One would have expected the king to be more cautious and not make such a public display of destroying the scroll, especially since three of his counselors begged him not to do it, fearing the consequences. We can only conclude that the king believed that as long as the scroll remained intact his fate was sealed, and the only way to undo the prophecy directed against him was to destroy the scroll it was written on. He had to show his counselors that the prophet's scroll was not a divine instrument, but rather a plain piece of parchment, which he, the king, could cut up and burn. Clearly, he was not acting rationally, and at least some of his men must have realized he was going to be punished for his action.

God orders Jeremiah to produce a new scroll and record everything that was written in the first scroll. Again, with the help of his faithful scribe, Jeremiah dictates the same prophecies and adds "many more such things" (36:32). What are those things? This phrase may very well be alluding to the long-term project the prophet and his disciple were engaged in, of not only recording Jeremiah's prophecies, but also in doing what the prophet considered of supreme importance, namely, assembling both written and oral material to create the final version of the book of Deuteronomy and the history of the conquest of Canaan by Joshua, the period of the judges, and the chronicle of the House of David, written in the spirit of the covenant between God and Israel, to show how the cumulative effect of Israel's failing to live up to the covenant is now reflected in the prophecies of Jeremiah, and providing us with the only history left of that period of some six centuries.[10]

In other words, Jeremiah and Baruch took the first major step in the process of assembling and finalizing those books of the Hebrew Bible that would enable Ezra the Scribe and Nehemiah and those who returned from Babylonian exile about a century later to reestablish a Torah-centered Jewish life in Jerusalem. When the Torah is quoted by those leaders to determine the status of non-Jews in the renewed Jewish community, they quote the words, "An Ammonite and a Moabite shall not enter the assembly of God" (Nehemiah 13:1), which is a direct quote from Deuteronomy (23:4), the book they received from Jeremiah and Baruch.

One may wonder why there is no mention in the book of Jeremiah or anywhere else in the Bible of Jeremiah and Baruch playing such a critical role in preserving the Torah or in writing down the post-Exodus history. In fact, when Ezra and Nehemiah refer to the Torah they have brought back with them from Babylonia, they call it the "Torah of Moses the man of God" (Ezra 3:2). By doing so, they officially attribute the books of the Torah to Moses, and this remains the traditional Jewish belief to this day. That Ezra knew about the prophet Jeremiah is attested by the opening verse of his book, where he starts out by saying,

> In the first year of Cyrus king of Persia, that the word of
> Adonai spoken by Jeremiah might be accomplished,
> Adonai stirred the spirit of Cyrus king of Persia that
> he made a proclamation throughout all his kingdom,
> and put it also in writing saying, Thus said Cyrus king of
> Persia, Adonai the God of Heaven gave me all the
> kingdoms of the earth and ordered me to build Him
> a house in Jerusalem, which is in Judah." (Ezra 1:1)

Jeremiah, then, is officially accepted as the one who predicted the return from Babylonia, but there is no mention of him preserving the Torah. Why? The answer may be this: The Jewish people under the leadership of Ezra and Nehemiah are undergoing a profound change, as a few thousands of them return to their ancestral land under very precarious conditions. They are reinventing themselves as a monotheistic nation ready to reconnect with their God and with the beginnings of their history. The Torah is now presented to them as the book they and their descendants will live by so that they may be protected by their God and dwell safely on their land. It is necessary that a text with such authority be attributed directly to Moses, who received it directly from God, rather than the result of a final redaction that took place less than a century earlier. No doubt, Jeremiah and Baruch felt the same way about it. To them it was also an ancient tradition they were writing down and passing on, albeit in the spirit of their time.

One further point can be made here. It is entirely possible that during the Babylonian exile the text assembled by Baruch and Jeremiah underwent further redactions. It might have been necessary to embellish the stories of the exodus and of the kingdoms of David and Solomon in order to present the exiles with a glorious past, a past worth aspiring to as a model for the future, in preparation for the next exodus, this time from Babylon back to Jerusalem. It is best left to one's disposition to accept or reject such things as miracles, as for example the splitting of the Red Sea, and to let each reader of the Bible decide to what extent the text is literal rather than figurative. Present-day archeologists, however, have revised the thinking of their predecessors who date back to the beginnings of systematic biblical archeology earlier in the twentieth century, and are questioning the magnitude of the Davidic and Solomonic empires.[11] The Bible is indeed a work in progress, and much is yet to be discovered.

15.

The First Exile

When God orders Jeremiah to write a second scroll, God also pronounces a severe punishment for Jehoiakim king of Judah and his subjects:

> Therefore thus says Adonai regarding Jehoiakim
> king of Judah:
> He shall not have a successor to sit on the throne
> of David, and his dead body shall be cast out and
> exposed to the heat in the daytime and at night
> to the frost.
> And I will punish him and his seed and his servants
> for their iniquity, And I will bring upon them,
> and upon all the inhabitants of Jerusalem
> And upon all the men of Judah all the evil that
> I have pronounced against them but they did
> not listen. (36:30-31)

The message is clear: By destroying the scroll, which contained the word of God, the king sealed his fate and the fate of his people. Destruction and exile are inevitable, which, indeed, is what happens eighteen years later. The problem is that, contrary to this prophecy, we are told in the Second Book of Kings that Jehoiakim "slept with his fathers, and his son Jehoiachin succeeded him as king" (24:6).

On the face of it, Jeremiah either overreacted or misunderstood the divine message. David Kimchi, the twelfth century Jewish commentator, explains the seeming contradiction by arguing that (a) the text does not mention that Jehoiakim was actually buried (as it does regarding his father, Josiah), because the Babylonians, who arrived three months later in Jerusalem, and against whom he had recently rebelled, refused him proper burial; and (b) his son, Jehoiachin, only ruled for three months, which means that he did not actually establish his reign. Rashi, writing a century earlier, points to the fact that the next chapter (37) begins with the story of King Zedekiah, skipping over Jehoiachin, "Because it came to show that the calamities he [Jeremiah] prophesied were fulfilled."

Clearly, Jeremiah read the situation correctly in terms of the final outcome. It makes perfect sense that the Babylonians, who did come to punish Jehoiakim for stopping to pay tribute and to make an example of him for their other vassal nations to see, arrived soon after he died and was laid to rest in the royal burial ground, and all they could do was take out his body and defile it. The other question, however, remains open: Even though Kimchi and Rashi explain it away by arguing that Jehoiachin, who only ruled for three months, cannot be considered a bona fide king, he is indeed listed as one of the last kings of Judah. Does it mean, then, that Jeremiah was editorializing?

As we have seen in the case of "the enemy from the north," the prophet is not a future-teller who has a crystal ball in which he can see future events down to the last detail. He is a visionary who is able to see the future consequences of present events and present human actions. What makes him a true prophet is the fact that he reads the events of his time correctly and he is vindicated by their consequences. In his state of mental agitation, he often engages in excessive language. As was discussed earlier in regard to what it means to "hear God's voice," the prophet does not necessarily hear a voice in the human sense, but rather has the ability to receive a divine message, which he, in turn, must articulate in human terms.

During the short reign of Jehoiachin we witness the beginning of the end of the Judean monarchy. We may recall that after the death of King Josiah, his elected successor, Jehoahaz, only reigned for three months when the Pharaoh's emissaries arrived in Jerusalem, deposed him and exiled him to Egypt, and put Jehoiakim in his place. Now we have history repeating itself, as Jehoiakim's son, Jehoiachin, also rules for three months when the Babylonians arrive in Jerusalem, depose him, and crown his uncle Zedekiah in his place.

It is at this point in time that one of the most famous and prominent emperors of antiquity appears in Jerusalem. His name is Nebuchadnezzar II, son of Nabopolassar, of Babylonia. He reigns from about 605 to 562 BCE. He is a brilliant general, a builder famous for his Hanging Gardens of Babylonia, one of the seven wonders of the ancient world, and a monarch who for the most part was a benevolent and enlightened ruler, especially in comparison to the Assyrian emperors who ruled before him and were notoriously ruthless. But he is best remembered in history as the evil king who destroyed Jerusalem and the Temple, and is one of the arch-villains of biblical history.

In all objectivity, this emperor gave the little kingdom of Judah several chances. Jehoiakim rebelled against him twice. Jehoiachin did not do anything to remedy the situation. When the Babylonians arrive in Jerusalem, they do not set the city on fire or destroy the Temple. Instead, they take the eighteen-year-old Jehoiachin, his mother (who probably at this point was the acting monarch), and the rest of the court, along with the ruling class, the soldiers and all the craftsmen and the smiths, a total of some ten thousand people, and exile them to Babylonia. We recall that among them was a young boy named Ezekiel, who will become, while in Babylonian exile, Jeremiah's spiritual heir. It is not until a few years later, when the last king of Judah, Zedekiah, once again rebels against him, that Nebuchadnezzar, who runs a vast empire and looks upon Judah as a small yet highly troublesome province, finally decided to destroy the city and put an end to the Davidic dynasty.

Soon after the exile of Jehoiachin, Jeremiah is free to go back to the Temple. He walks up the hill from his home to the Temple Mount, and as he reaches the grounds of the House of God, he sees two baskets of figs. He is struck by the fact that the figs in one basket are plump and succulent, while the ones in the other basket are shriveled and inedible. He hears the voice of God:

> And Adonai said to me:
> What do you see, Jeremiah?
> And I said: Figs. The good figs are very good,
> and the bad figs are very bad, so bad they are inedible.
> And the word of Adonai came to me saying:
> Thus said Adonai God of Israel:
> Like the good figs, I will look favorably upon
> the exiles of Judah whom I have
> sent out of this place. I will look after them
> favorably and I will bring them back to this
> land and rebuild them and will not destroy them,
> and replant them and will not uproot them.
> And I will give them a heart that knows that
> I am God and they will be My people
> and I will be their God,
> for they will return to Me with all their heart.
> And like the bad figs, which are inedible,
> says Adonai, so will I abandon Zedekiah
> king of Judah and his officials,
> and the remnant of Jerusalem who remain in
> this land and the ones who dwell in the
> land of Egypt.
> I will make them a terror and an evil
> for all the kingdoms of the earth,
> as a reproach and a proverb,
> a taunt and a curse in all the places where
> I will scatter them. I will send the sword,
> famine and the pestilence
> upon them until they are destroyed

from the land which I gave
to them and their forefathers. (24:3-10)

Clearly, the best and the brightest had been exiled to Babylonia, including such luminaries as Ezekiel and Daniel. The dross was left behind and, to make things worse, the new king, Zedekiah, was obviously no Josiah. What is also interesting is that Jeremiah makes it clear he has no use for the earlier Judean exiles who had been sent to Egypt after the death of Josiah, where they reintroduced their idolatrous practices.

16.

Nebuchadnezzar as God's Instrument

One of the most interesting paradoxes about Jeremiah is his attitude towards Nebuchadnezzar. For years he anticipates that "trouble will come from the north," and as a result he has horrific visions of mighty armies swooping down from the north, riding their swift horses and destroying everything in their path. When this mysterious enemy finally acquires an identity and turns out to be the Babylonian emperor Nebuchadnezzar, the prophet does not react with horror. Instead, he seems to be calmly accepting the premise that this archenemy is the inevitable instrument of God's will, with whom one must deal not as someone who will exterminate the Jewish people, but rather facilitate their transition to the next stage of their history, indeed to the enduring pattern of their existence.

This is something which his contemporaries did not understand, and for which, as we shall see, they will persecute him severely.

Jeremiah realizes that the days of the kingdom of Judah are numbered. It is clear to him that any attempt to overthrow the yoke of Babylonia can only result in disaster. He accepts the reality of living under Babylonian rule, and he knows that this rule is short-lived. Most important, he accepts Nebuchadnezzar as the instrument of God, whom God uses to punish his wayward children. The prophet understands the rise and fall of empires, and the special role his people will have to play on the stage of history as witnesses to the one God of the Universe. Eventually, his people will also begin to understand these things, but for now they are not aware of them. Jeremiah's timeframe is the future; theirs is the present.

At one point Jeremiah says:

> At that time they will call Jerusalem the seat of Adonai,
> And all the nations will gather there for the sake of
> Adonai in Jerusalem. And they will no longer follow
> The stubbornness of their evil heart. (3:17)

Here Jeremiah is looking far into the future. He sees Jerusalem a thousand years after his time, when it becomes the center of world religions. One could argue that the first part of this prophecy has been fulfilled, namely, Jerusalem has become the city not only of the Hebrew prophets, but also the place where Christianity was born, and where Islam's founder went up to heaven. The second part, "And they will no longer follow the stubbornness of their evil heart," is yet to happen.

God first appears to Jeremiah in nature, but what becomes central to the prophet's teaching is the way God operates in history. Human history is not merely the result of human actions and decisions, whether economic, social, cultural or military. There is a higher force that guides human affairs, and there is a purpose to the way history evolves. In Einstein's famous words, "God does not play dice with the universe." While some people may disagree with this point of view, there is one objective lesson we all learn from human history, over and over again: Human evil carries within itself the seeds of its own destruction. Whether one attributes this to a higher power or to sociological laws, it still remains one of the constants of human history.

17.

Jeremiah and the Reign of Zedekiah

Zedekiah is the last king of Judah. His original name was Mattaniah, Hebrew for "gift of God" (II Kings 24:17). When Nebuchadnezzar exiles Jehoiachin and puts his uncle Mattaniah in his place, he renames him Zedekiah, Hebrew for "God is my righteousness." With names like these, one is inclined to think of this king as pious and righteous, but it turns out that he was neither. Like his brother Jehoiakim and his nephew Jehoiachin, he "does that which is evil in the eyes of Adonai" (24:19). But there is a vast difference between him and his brother. As we saw in the story of the burning of the scroll, Jehoiakim was a decisive ruler who was completely sure of himself, while Zedekiah is consumed with doubts, unable to make up his mind, and at the mercy of his advisors. His behavior must have infuriated his Babylonian patron to such a degree that it finally resulted in the destruction of Jerusalem and in Zedekiah being punished more severely than anyone else in the Bible.

Ironically, Zedekiah in his indecisiveness is the first of the five kings under whom Jeremiah lived who in effect elevates him to the rank of court prophet, an honor Jeremiah would rather do without. The last thing in the world Jeremiah wants to be is a court prophet. During his long life, Jeremiah never met a court prophet who spoke truth to power. They were all false prophets or, to use the exact Hebrew term, lying prophets. Jeremiah was certainly not going to lie to the king and, needless to say, his troubles, which were never few, now take a turn for the worse.

Under Zedekiah, Jeremiah is not only recognized as a legitimate prophet of the God of Israel, but he is actually being personally consulted by the king. This is a major turning point in his prophetic career. The only problem is, Zedekiah does not want to hear the truth. He wants Jeremiah to be a typical court prophet, namely, a yes-man. Needless to say, he has picked the wrong person. Jeremiah has no illusions about Zedekiah. It is clear to him Zedekiah is the wrong man at the wrong time. In fact, it is as if God had picked this weak monarch on purpose, knowing that it is too late for the kingdom to be saved. Jeremiah realizes that things are only going to get worse.

He begins to wonder why God picked him to be a prophet of doom, a harbinger of the terrible fate awaiting his people. He cries out to God in his despair:

> You have seduced me, Adonai, and I was seduced.
> You have overcome me, and have prevailed.
> I have become the laughingstock all day long,

Everyone is mocking me.
And if I say: I will not make mention of Him,
Nor speak any more in His name,
Then there is in my heart as it were a
Burning fire shut up in my bones,
And I weary myself to hold it in, but cannot.
(20:7-9)

Clearly, the prophet wishes he could stop prophesying or give up his mission altogether. But there is no way out. He must go on all the way to the bitter end, which now seems close at hand. Jeremiah is a man of strong words, and when he tells God "You have seduced me," he is certainly not holding anything back. But when he goes on to say, "burning fire shut up in my bones," it is clear that he is in great pain, and rather than turn his back on God he tells God exactly how he feels without losing any of his faith and without stopping for a moment to act like a prophet.

For about eight years Zedekiah accepts the yoke of Babylonia, and rules as a vassal king. During those eight years his nephew, ousted king Jehoiachin, along with his mother, his counselors, and the Jerusalem elite, lives in Babylonian exile. Jehoiachin and those around him continues to have a say in the affairs of Jerusalem, and in effect at this point the center of Jewish life begins to shift from Jerusalem to Babylonia in a way that will affect the future of Judaism (it is interesting to note that the same did not happen with the previous exile to Egypt a few years earlier). Jeremiah, as we shall see, becomes active in supporting the community in Babylonia, which he knows holds the key to the future.

18.

The Prophet Hananiah and the Yoke

The role of the prophet is never clear in the Bible. As we follow Jeremiah's prophetic career, we see it change and evolve. From a chastiser inveighing against idolatry and immorality, he becomes a teacher of the law and an editor of the biblical text. He then becomes a political activist. From an anti-establishment voice of conscience, he becomes a court prophet when, in reality, he remains an outsider who gives the court no comfort. Finally, from a prophet of doom he will become a prophet of consolation.

All these roles come into play during the time of Zedekiah. Jeremiah goes through his mood swings, living, it seems, in a constant state of emotional upheaval, and yet he finds the time and the energy to accomplish more than most people have ever accomplished. One wonders whether he realized he was playing such a critical role in the history of his people (and the world), given his self-deprecation and self-pity.

In the fourth year of the reign of King Zedekiah, something was happening in the Babylonian Empire that forced its emperor to shift his attention from Judah and its neighbors to other parts of his empire. It might have been an uprising somewhere in Mesopotamia. Zedekiah, encouraged by a new Pharaoh in Egypt, decided to call a meeting in Jerusalem of the kings of his neighboring nations, all of whom were living under the Babylonian yoke, and plot a joint uprising against their patron. Jeremiah was vehemently opposed to this undertaking, and since the king, his counselors, and the other court prophets would not listen to him, he decided to resort to his old methods of dramatizing his message.

God says to Jeremiah:

> Make yourself bands and bars, and put them
> on your neck; and send them to the king of Edom,
> and to the king of Moab, and to the king of the
> children of Ammon, and to the king of Tyre,
> and to the king of Zidon, by the hand of the
> messengers that come to Jerusalem to
> Zedekiah king of Judah; and give them a
> charge to their masters, saying: Thus says Adonai
> of hosts, the God of Israel: You shall say to
> your masters: I have made the earth and man
> and beast upon the face of the earth,
> by My great power and by My outstretched arm;

and I give it to whom it seems right to Me.
And now have I given all these lands into the
hand of Nebuchadnezzar king of Babylon,
My servant; and the beasts of the field also
have I given him to serve him. And all the nations
shall serve him, and his son, and his son's son,
until the time of his own land come;
and then many nations and great kings shall
make him their servant. (27:2-7)

Here, for the first time, we see Jeremiah carrying his prophetic activities to other nations, in keeping with his original charge to become "a prophet to the nations" (1:5). He refers to Nebuchadnezzar as "God's servant," rather than something on the order of the "great Satan," as small nations today would sometimes refer to a world power. Elsewhere in the Bible, Israel is referred to as "Jacob My servant." The implication in both cases is clear: No one can defeat someone whom God has chosen as God's servant, whether a small nation or a world power. At the same time, God did not enter into any covenant with the Babylonian king, hence his time will come, and he too, like other world powers before him, will become a servant.

As it turns out, the uprising did not take place, and we read later on (51:59) that Zedekiah sent a certain delegation to Babylonia that year, which very well could have been a show of obedience to Nebuchadnezzar. It is rather doubtful that Jeremiah parading in the streets of Jerusalem with bands and bars on his neck swayed this alliance to desist from rebelling. More likely they realized that their efforts would be futile.

But this is not the end of this story.

While Jeremiah was roaming the streets with his strange gear, another prophet named Hananiah son of Azur, the prophet from Gibeon, shows up at the Temple and tells Jeremiah in front of the priests and the rest of the people:

Thus spoke Adonai of hosts, the God of Israel, saying:
I have broken the yoke of the king of Babylon.
Within two full years will I bring back into this place
all the vessels of Adonai's house which Nebuchadnezzar
king of Babylon took away from this place,
and carried them to Babylon; and I will bring back
to this place Jeconiah the son of Jehoiakim,
king of Judah, with all the captives of Judah,
that went to Babylon, says Adonai;
for I will break the yoke of the king of Babylon. (28:3-4)

It is clear to Jeremiah that God would not give him one message, and another prophet a conflicting message. Hananiah, in effect, is challenging the veracity of Jeremiah's prophecy about the continuing subjugation to Babylonia. The bands and bars Jeremiah is wearing on his neck are a misrepresentation, Hananiah seems to be saying. Jeremiah does not lose his composure. He says to Hananiah in front of the assemblage,

> Then the prophet Jeremiah said to the
> prophet Hananiah in the presence of the priests,
> and in the presence of all the
> people that stood in the house of Adonai,
> even the prophet Jeremiah said:
> Amen! May Adonai do so!
> May Adonai perform your words
> that you have prophesied,
> to bring back the vessels of Adonai's house,
> and all those who were carried
> away captive, from Babylon to this place!
> Nevertheless hear now this word that I speak
> in your ears, and in the ears of all the people:
> The prophets that have been before me and
> before you of old prophesied against many countries,
> and against great kingdoms, of war, and of evil,
> and of pestilence. The prophet that would
> prophesy peace, when the word of that prophet
> shall come to pass, then shall the prophet be known,
> that Adonai truly sent him. (28:5-9)

This is one of the most revealing episodes in the entire Bible concerning the nature and the validity of prophecy. Jeremiah does not call Hananiah a false prophet, as he is quick to call so many of the other so-called prophets of his time. The biblical text repeatedly refers to Hananiah as prophet, and Hananiah uses the familiar formula of "thus says Adonai" when he prophesies. Jeremiah goes so far as to say to Hananiah what amounts to, "From your mouth to God's ear." This is something Jeremiah never says to any other prophet. And then Jeremiah makes his concluding statement, which provides the key to what makes a prophet truly a prophet: It takes courage, Jeremiah seems to argue, for a prophet to bring bad news. But when a prophet brings good news, which is what court prophets routinely do, then the good news must first turn out to be true before the prophet is pronounced a true prophet. In other words, Jeremiah, albeit in a friendly way, questions Hananiah's prophetic authority. Most likely, Hananiah was yet to prove himself a true prophet, while Jeremiah has now been a prophet for about thirty years, and more than a few of his prophecies have been fulfilled. Hananiah is not about to give up:

> Then Hananiah the prophet took the bar from
> off the prophet Jeremiah's neck, and broke it.
> And Hananiah spoke in the presence of all the people,
> saying: Thus says Adonai: Even so will I break the yoke
> of Nebuchadnezzar king of Babylon from off the neck of
> all the nations within two full years. And the prophet
> Jeremiah went on his way. (28:10-11)

But Jeremiah does not give up either. God orders him to replace the wooden bars with a new set made of iron, which cannot be broken. Jeremiah returns to the Temple with his new yoke, and tells Hananiah that because of his false promises to the people, God decided to strike him dead within a year. Two months later, Hananiah dies. Why and how he dies we are not told. The biblical writer seems to imply that the story needs no further elaboration.

19.

"Ask for the Peace of the City"

What makes Jeremiah a great prophet is not only his ability to see the future, but his quick grasp of events in the present, from which he derives long-term lessons. The best case in point is his understanding of the diaspora, a dominant aspect of Jewish history, which begins in his lifetime and continues to this day. It is clear that to his contemporaries, as we saw in the story of the prophet Hananiah, it was inconceivable that Jewish life could exist outside the land of Israel. What seemed to be the consensus among the people who remained in Judah after the exile of Jehoiachin (the exile prior to the final one) was that the exiles in Babylonia were captive people, and before long either God would bring them back or they would become assimilated and disappear altogether.

Jeremiah knew better. He understood that since God is neither tribal nor territorial, the people with whom God made the covenant are not limited to one small corner of the earth. While the land of Israel—which he loved passionately— is the land God promised to Moses as both the physical and the spiritual home for his people, it was possible to live in places like Egypt or Babylonia and still maintain a Jewish life, resist idolatry, and worship God. After all, Moses himself was born in Egypt and raised in the court of the Pharaoh, and Abraham was born in Babylonia to a father who, according to Jewish legend, was an idol maker. Jeremiah does not accept the Diaspora as permanent, but he realizes that it can exist for long periods of time and that the covenant has the power to outlive it.

It is important to bear in mind that once the people of Israel (the Northern Kingdom) and Judah (the Southern Kingdom) arrive in either Egypt or Babylonia, they encounter pagan civilizations far more magnificent than the Canaanite one of the former inhabitants of their land and the small surrounding nations such as the Phoenicians, the Philistines, the Edomites etc. The physical remains of the Egyptian and Babylonian civilizations can still be found in present-day Egypt and Iraq, and we are still overwhelmed by the ziggurats of Mesopotamia and the pyramids, temples and gigantic statues and monuments in Giza, Luxor, and many other places in Egypt. Needless to say, in the days of Nebuchadnezzar II the Judean exiles encountered the famous hanging gardens and other architectural wonders as they came face to face with the center of power of the Babylonian empire.

Jeremiah must have been aware of all of this, and he knew that his fight against idolatry in Jerusalem took on an even greater urgency in regard to the new diaspora communities in Egypt and Babylonia. We only have a few short references in his book to this problem, but we can piece together a fairly accurate picture of how he dealt with it.

There is one single verse in his book which is not written in Hebrew but rather in Aramaic, the lingua franca of his time, which was spoken throughout the ancient Near East, including Mesopotamia:

> Kidnah teymrun lehon: elohayah di-shemayah vearkah
> la aveydu yeveydu meyarah umin tehot shemayah eyleh.

> (Thus shall you say to them:
> The gods that have not made the
> heavens and the earth,
> these shall perish from the earth,
> and from under the heavens. [10:11])

Clearly, he is not speaking to the people in Judah, whose language is Hebrew. The verse stands alone in the text as if it were inserted from a different source. Nor is it God talking to Jeremiah, since God always speaks to him in Hebrew. It is Jeremiah addressing an emissary sent to the Diaspora, either verbally or in one of the many letters he started to send at that time to his exiled brethren. He wants to make sure that even the children, who are now speaking Aramaic rather than Hebrew, or the non-Jews who are now joining the Jewish community (see Ezra and Nehemiah), understand it. He is providing, so to speak, a mantra which he wants them to memorize and keep repeating as they gaze upon the giant monuments of the pagan world and are tempted to follow its pagan gods:

> The gods that have not made the heavens
> and the earth shall perish from the earth and
> from under the heavens.

You, Judeans, on the other hand, have the only true and everlasting God, while these are objects of wood and stone.

We recall that when the king plots an uprising with his neighbors, he sends a delegation to Babylonia to appease his patron and assure him of his loyalty. Jeremiah takes advantage of the opportunity and sends a written message to "the elders and the priests and the prophets and all the people whom Nebuchadnezzar has exiled to Babylonia," (29:1), in which he writes:

> Thus says Adonai of hosts, the God of Israel,
> to all the captivity, whom I have caused to be

carried away captive from Jerusalem unto Babylon:
Build yourselves houses, and dwell in them,
and plant gardens, and eat their fruit; take wives,
and beget sons and daughters;
and take wives for your sons, and give your
daughters to husbands, that they may bear
sons and daughters; and multiply there,
and be not diminished. And ask for the
peace of the city whither I have caused you
to be carried away captive, and pray to Adonai for it;
for in its peace shall you have peace. (29:4-7)

Certainly the king did not give his approval to this message, since he, like the rest of the people, did not see the exile as a long-term affair. Once again, Jeremiah is defying his patrons, this time making use of an official court delegation to carry his own message. And once again, he gets away with it, although we shall soon find out that he is asking for trouble, as he has always done in the past. Perhaps the most interesting statement in this epistle to the exiled Jews is the phrase: "Ask for the peace of the city." He is telling the exiles, in effect, to be good loyal citizens of their new country.[12] At the same time, he goes on to say:

For thus says Adonai: When Babylon completes
seventy years I will remember you,
and perform My good word on your behalf,
in causing you to return to this place.
For I know the thoughts that I think about you,
says Adonai, are thoughts of peace,
and not of evil, to give you a future and a hope.[13]
(29:10-11)

The use of the number seventy is poetic, and if we put it together with the previous quote, it refers to a period of time covering three generations, as Jeremiah speaks about the exiles' children and grandchildren, after which time the return to Zion will take place.

Thus Jeremiah launches his campaign to preserve Judaism in the Diaspora, and looks upon the Babylonian exiles as the people who will restore Judaism in Jerusalem when the time comes, as indeed happens some seventy years later in the time of Ezra and Nehemiah. He then turns to his fellow Judeans who are left in Judah and reminds them that their fate is sealed as they await destruction:

> For thus says Adonai concerning the king that sits
> upon the throne of David, and concerning all the people
> that dwell in this city, your brethren who did not go
> with you into captivity; thus says Adonai of hosts:
> Behold, I will send upon them the sword, the famine,
> and the pestilence, and will make them like vile figs,
> that cannot be eaten, they are so bad. (29:16-17)

While Jeremiah is busy sending messages of hope and good counsel to the Judeans in Babylonia, he has to combat those false court prophets who were sent there with King Jehoiachin, and were apparently doing their best to discredit him. On two of them, Ahab son of Kolaiah, and Zedekiah son of Maaseiah, he puts a curse, having found out that they engaged in adultery (29:23). It appears they were burned alive (see book of Daniel regarding this practice), and Jeremiah uses them as an object lesson.

A third false prophet named Shemaiah the Nehelamite sends word to Jerusalem to a priest named Zephaniah son of Maaseiah, in which he denounces Jeremiah and says:

> Adonai has made you priest instead of
> Jehoiadah the priest, that there should be
> officers in the house of Adonai for every
> man that is mad, and makes himself a prophet,
> that you should put him in the stocks and in prison.
> Now therefore, why have you not rebuked Jeremiah
> of Anathoth, who makes himself a prophet to you,
> forasmuch as he has sent to us in Babylon, saying:
> The captivity is long; build yourselves houses,
> and dwell in them; and plant gardens, and eat their fruit?
> (29:26-28)

The message is delivered to Zephaniah the priest who summons Jeremiah and reads it to him. We are not told what the consequences were, but it is interesting to note that Shemaiah the Nehelamite questions Jeremiah's credentials as a prophet of the God of Israel even at this late date. Furthermore, the suggestion he makes about incarcerating Jeremiah and making an example of him will not go unheeded when the time comes.

20.

Like Clay in the Hands of the Potter

One day Jeremiah stops at the shop of a potter who is making clay pots. The potter is fashioning the vessel from soft clay, shaping it with his hands. Every once in a while the potter's hand slips and spoils the shape of the vessel. The potter then presses the clay into a lump and starts over again, shaping a new vessel.

As he observes the potter, Jeremiah hears the voice of God speaking to him, telling him that the House of Israel is like clay in the hands of God. God is the potter who can create and destroy and create again. Jeremiah goes to the Temple and tells the people the parable of the potter. But the people are not interested. They have heard how he had been praising the exiles in Babylonia and has been denouncing them as "vile figs." They complain about him to the priests and the prophets in the Temple, who respond by saying:

> Come, and let us outsmart Jeremiah;
> for instruction shall not perish from the priest,
> nor counsel from the wise,
> nor the word from the prophet.
> Come, and let us smite him with the tongue,
> and let us not give heed to any of his words.
> (18:18)

Jeremiah realizes that his message was too mild, and that the people are too far-gone in their rebelliousness against God. Again he looks for a sign from God, when he is told:

> Thus says Adonai: Go, and get a potter's earthen bottle,
> and take of the elders of the people,
> and of the elders of the priests;
> and go forth to the valley of the son of Hinnom,
> which is by the entry of the gate Harsith,
> and proclaim there the words that I shall tell you;
> and say: Hear the word of Adonai,
> O kings of Judah, and inhabitants of Jerusalem;
> thus says Adonai of hosts, the God of Israel:
> Behold, I will bring evil upon this place,

that whoever hears it his ears shall tingle. . . .
(19:1-3)

Jeremiah takes along with him a group of elders as well as senior priests, who he hopes will be duly impressed by his prophecy and will try to bring the people back to God. He takes them to the place outside Jerusalem where some of the worst acts of idolatry have taken place over the years, including human sacrifice, and he proceeds to pronounce one of the most shocking of all his prophecies:

> Therefore, behold, the days come, says Adonai,
> that this place shall no more be called Topheth,
> nor the valley of the son of Hinnom,
> but the valley of slaughter; and I will make void
> the counsel of Judah and Jerusalem in this place;
> and I will cause them to fall by the sword before
> their enemies, and by the hand of them that
> seek their life; and their carcasses will I give
> to be food for the fowls of the heaven,
> and for the beasts of the earth;
> and I will make this city an astonishment,
> and a hissing; every one that passes thereby
> shall be astonished and hiss because of all
> the plagues thereof. . . . (19:6-8)

Jeremiah proceeds to break the earthen bottle he has brought with him, and tells the elders this is how God is going to destroy the people and the city, where so many are going to die that there will be no room to bury them.

We are not told how the elders reacted to this dire prophecy. Instead, we are told that Jeremiah had to go to the Temple courtyard himself and repeat his prophecy there. It is not hard to guess that he achieved the opposite results of what he had expected:

> Now Pashhur the son of Immer the priest,
> who was chief officer in the house of Adonai,
> heard Jeremiah prophesying these things.
> Then Pashhur smote Jeremiah the prophet,
> and put him in the stocks that were in the
> upper gate of Benjamin, which was in the

house of Adonai. And it happened the next
day that Pashhur brought forth Jeremiah out
of the stocks. Then said Jeremiah to him:
Adonai has not called your name Pashhur,
but Magormissabib. (20:1-3)

Jeremiah, in other words, is subjected to a bodily punishment, which most likely consisted of forty lashes, and is kept overnight in prison where he suffers physical pain that prevents him from getting any sleep. When he is released in the morning, he puts a curse on Pashhur, letting him know that he will lose all his loved ones when the enemy arrives in Jerusalem (*magormissabib* is Hebrew for terror all around).[14]

When Jeremiah comes out of jail, he gives praise to God for having once again saved his life:

Sing to Adonai, praise Adonai;
For He has delivered the soul of the humble
From the hand of evildoers. (20:13)

What next? Jeremiah wonders. Yes, he has survived, but for what purpose? He is now being treated like a common criminal, and yet he cannot do anything about it. He will continue to chastise these people, and they will continue to persecute him. Where does it end?

To add to his woes, Jeremiah receives word from Anathoth that his old mother died. He recalls the time she came to see him in Jerusalem and tried to talk him into rejoining the priesthood. He thinks of how he had let down his father, the priest Hilkiah, and made his mother unhappy. Did not God say, "Honor your father and your mother?"

It is then that Jeremiah, who was called forth from the womb to be a prophet, curses the day of his birth:

Cursed be the day I was born,
Let not the day my mother bore me be blessed.
Cursed be the man who told my father
A male child is born to you, giving him such joy!
Let him be like the cities Adonai overthrew,
unrelenting,
Let him hear shrieks in the morning
And battle shouts at noontide.
For I did not die in the womb

So that my mother might be my grave,
And her womb my resting place for all time.
Why did I ever come out of the womb
To see misery and pain
And to end my days in shame? (20:14-18)[15]

21.

The Siege of Jerusalem

In the eighth year of his reign, Zedekiah decides to, or, more precisely, his advisors talk him into rebelling against Babylonia. This sets the scene for the great catastrophe that will forever change the destiny of his people, and would remove the House of David from the throne to this day. Jeremiah is now reaching his old age. He would like to retire to Anathoth and end his days in peace. But it is not meant to be. He has to campaign against the decision to go to war. He is weary of the king and of the people left in Judah. Yet he has no thoughts of going to Babylon, where the exiles who he believes hold the key for the future of Israel now live. He is getting too old, and he wishes to remain in his native land no matter what. Moreover, he and Baruch are engaged in their long-term project of assembling and writing the Torah, which takes a great deal of their time.

Zedekiah makes an alliance with Pharaoh Hophra, king of Egypt, in the belief that together they can overthrow the yoke of Nebuchadnezzar. A few months later, the Babylonian army lays siege to Jerusalem. The Egyptians send their army to engage the Babylonians in battle, and the Babylonians decide to retreat from Jerusalem and do battle with the Egyptians. Zedekiah, however, starts having second thoughts about the revolt. He is not satisfied with the advice he gets from his generals and court prophets, so he solicits Jeremiah's help in the hope of receiving reassurance from the God of Israel.

> Now Zedekiah the son of Josiah whom Nebuchadnezzar
> king of Babylon had made king in the land of Judah,
> reigned as king in place of Coniah [Jehoiachin]
> the son of Jehoiakim. But neither he nor his servants
> nor the people of the land listened to the words of
> Adonai which He spoke through Jeremiah the prophet.
> Yet King Zedekiah sent Jehucal the son of Shelemiah,[16]
> and Zephaniah the son of Maaseiah, the priest,
> to Jeremiah the prophet, saying,
> "Please pray to Adonai our God on our behalf." (37:1-3)

Jeremiah knows what they want to hear. They would like God to repeat the miracle of the time of King Hezekiah, when the Assyrians under Senacherib laid siege to Jerusalem and, in the middle of the night, an angel of God came down from heaven and slew all the Assyrians. Don't expect a miracle, Jeremiah says.

Even if you defeat the whole Babylonian army and they all lie wounded in their tents, they will still rise and burn down this city.

In this statement Jeremiah seems to be investing the Babylonians with super-human powers. The implication is clear: When King Hezekiah, the ancestor of Zedekiah, did "that which was right in the eyes of God," the prophet Isaiah assured him that God was on his side, and even though Judah's army was no match to the Assyrian forces, God performed a miracle to defeat the Assyrians. Here, on the other hand, the opposite is happening. Now God is on the side of Judah's enemy, which makes this enemy invincible.

This is an extremely harsh prophecy. Moreover, as we read this biblical text we seem to find ourselves not in the realm of history but rather in the realm of mythology. It would be easy to conclude that someone imagined these events, and that they have little to do with historical fact.

And yet, a remarkable archeological discovery dating back to 1935 and 1938 confirms a great deal of what was happening in Judah during the two years of the siege of Jerusalem. It is known as the Lachish Letters. It consists of sixteen bro-ken pieces of pottery known as ostraca, or inscribed potsherds, found by the Brit-ish archeologist J. L. Starkey in the ruins of the coastal town of Lachish, south-west of Jerusalem. The text on the ostraca represents communiqués between Zedekiah's garrison in Lachish and a small outpost on the western border of Judah. It is written in the Hebrew script of the period and in the style of the book of Jeremiah, and mentions the name Jeremiah as well as Coniah and other names of the period. It makes reference to a soldier who is sent to Egypt, presumably to make contact with the Egyptian army. It conveys the dire situation of the Lachish garrison, where the morale is low (Lachish is mentioned in the book of Jeremiah as one of the last outposts to hold out against the Babylonians [34:7]), and where the commander is concerned that the end is near. The Lachish Letters reinforce the historical validity of the book of Jeremiah as an accurate record of the last days of the kingdom of Judah.

While the siege is temporarily lifted during the arrival of the Egyptian army, Jerusa-lem is having a short reprieve. The defending army, however, is guarding the walls and the gates, fearing a surprise attack. Supplies are being brought into the city from the surrounding countryside, and some people try to take advantage of this opportunity to escape from the city. Jeremiah decides to go to Anathoth, presumably to attend to some family business related to his inherited property, and to visit his parents' graves. As he reaches the Benjamin Gate in the northern end of the city, the captain of the guard, Irijah son of Shelemiah, recognizes him.

What an honor, Irijah says with a derisive smile. To what do we owe this honor, Jeremiah? Have you come to tell us to surrender to the enemy?

I haven't come to tell you anything, Jeremiah says. I am going to Anathoth to take care of some family business.

No, you are not, Irijah says. You are going over to the enemy. I have heard you speak at the Temple. You are lucky they let you walk around free.

You are lying, Jeremiah replies. I am only going to Anathoth.

Seize him! Irijah orders his men. This man is a traitor. Take him to the king.

Jeremiah's hands are bound and he is taken back to the king's palace, where he is questioned by some of the king's officers. The officers refuse to believe his story. They are all young, and they show little respect for this old troublemaker whose words only help demoralize their soldiers.

We shouldn't take any chances, one of them says. We better detain him until we find out what his true intentions are.

It seems that a good number of people were being put into jail at that time, as more than a few were looking to escape from the city. The prisons are full, and some private homes are being converted into jails. Jeremiah is locked up at the home of Jonathan the scribe, where some members of the elite of Jerusalem's society are being held.

The old prophet is pronounced a menace to the public, and he is kept at the house of Jonathan the scribe for several months. While in jail he is frequently visited by his own scribe, Baruch, who continues to take dictation and write down prophecies and messages.

Shortly after Jeremiah was sent to jail, Baruch came to see him with some disturbing news. When Jerusalem first came under siege, it became clear that those in Jerusalem who owned Hebrew slaves did not have much need for them, since food supplies were scarce and movement was restricted. The army, on the other hand, needed more recruits for the defense of the city. The king issued a decree to free the Hebrew slaves. According to the law in Deuteronomy, a Hebrew slave had to be set free on the seventh year, but most people ignored this law. A special ceremony was held to mark this occasion and the king concluded a covenant with his people to set the slaves free. Then, when the siege was lifted during the approach of the Egyptian army, many people decided to ignore the covenant and forced the freed slaves back into slavery.

Jeremiah told Baruch to write a letter to the king, in which he said:

> Therefore thus says Adonai:
> You have not listened to Me, to proclaim liberty,
> every man to his brother, and every man to
> his neighbor; behold, I proclaim liberty,
> says Adonai, to the sword, to the pestilence,
> and to the famine; and I will make you a horror
> to all the kingdoms of the earth. (34:17)

One night Jeremiah is awakened in the middle of the night. He is given new clothes and told to wash up and get dressed as he is being taken to see an important person.

Can it wait till tomorrow? He asks.

No, you have to go immediately.

Under heavy guard he is taken to the king's palace, where he is left alone in a waiting room. After a while the door opens and in walks none other than the king. Zedekiah looks haggard, like a man who was not getting much sleep.

Jeremiah stands up and bows to the king.

Sit, sit, Zedekiah insists. They both sit down facing each other.

How is your majesty?

Not very well. Food is becoming scarce in the city, and I am not sure how long we can hold out.

There is still time, my lord the king. If you send a peace delegation to Nebuchadnezzar he will spare you and the city.

I can't. My men won't let me. They are determined to fight.

But you are the king!

It is too late.

Jeremiah does not say a word.

The king leans over and whispers in Jeremiah's ear,

Any word from your Master?

Yes. You will fall into the hands of the king of Babylon.

The king shakes his head. He forces a smile and asks,

Do they feed you well?

Barely. My lord, can I ask you a question?

Ask.

Why am I being punished? I did not do anything to you, or to your servants, or to the rest of the people that I should be sitting in jail. Where are the prophets who have predicted that the Babylonians would not invade this land? I beg of you, my lord the king, do not put me back in the house of Jonathan the scribe and leave me there to die.

> Then Zedekiah the king commanded, and they committed
> Jeremiah into the court of the guard, and they gave him a
> daily loaf of bread out of the bakers' street, until all the
> bread in the city was spent. Thus Jeremiah remained in the
> court of the guard. (37:21)

Jerusalem has now been under siege for about a year. Altogether, it will hold out against Nebuchadnezzar's forces for eighteen months. Keeping in mind that a few years earlier, during Jehoiachin's exile, the best and the brightest of Judah's society as well as its military leaders and expert craftsmen were exiled to Babylonia, and judging from the numbers of those who will eventually be exiled when the city falls (52:30), the population holding out against the enemy did not even number in the tens of thousands. And yet it was engaging the strongest army in the world, an army that during the siege was able to ward off an Egyptian force that came to the rescue of the Judeans. Clearly, the pro-Egyptian party in the city that believed it could win against the Babylonians knew that Jerusalem was one of the most fortified cities of its time; the Judeans were brave and skillful soldiers; and the empire they were facing was stretched too thin, constantly engaged in putting down uprisings at home and abroad. And, in the final analysis, was not invincible. Until the moment the walls of the city were finally breached, the members of the pro-Egyptian party had hope. Moreover, the God of Israel and of the universe dwelled in the Holy Temple in the heart of Jerusalem, and how would God allow His own house to be destroyed?

But God did not speak to the pro-Egyptian party, or to the court prophets, or to the priests, and certainly not to the king. God spoke to Jeremiah, who was being detained at the court of the guard. By now, Jeremiah's message about the inevitable fall of Jerusalem began to bear fruit, as a growing number of Judeans began to realize that the end was near, and that it would be better to surrender to the Babylonian emperor, who would in turn spare the city, rather than lose everything.

But it was too little too late. The king's generals were the leaders of the pro-Egyptian party, and they were determined to fight to the end. Jeremiah knew that the only chance left to save the kingdom was for Zedekiah to assert himself and to surrender to Nebuchadnezzar. Yes, he would be deposed, but his life would be spared, and his son would be made king in his place. Meanwhile, the siege was now entering its second year.

22.

Jeremiah and the Field in Anathoth

One day a visitor came to see Jeremiah at the court of the guard. It was his cousin Hanamel son of Shallum from Anathoth. He hadn't seen his cousin in years. When they were little boys they played together in the fields of Anathoth, and they were good friends. Hanamel's father, Shallum, was close to his brother, Hilkiah, Jeremiah's father. Even after Jeremiah left Anathoth and his own relatives turned against him, Hanamel remained his friend, and would secretly bring Jeremiah messages from his mother. Like Jeremiah, Hanamel was getting on in years, and was now living all alone on the family's land. The two cousins embraced. Hanamel looked at the old prophet and was visibly saddened to see his cousin held prisoner.

How were you able to get through the besieging army? Jeremiah asked.

I told them I was your cousin. They heard about that old prophet in the city who is trying to persuade the king to lay down his arms. They told me they were letting me through so I could go and talk to you. But this is not why I came.

Any news from Anathoth?

Well, I have to sell my field. I can no longer take care of it. But I want it to remain as part of our family's estate, so I thought you might want to buy it.

According to the book of Leviticus (25:25), "If your brother is in straits and has to sell part of his holding, his nearest redeemer shall come and redeem what his brother has sold." Jeremiah must have been Hanamel's nearest redeemer. The land must have been in the family for generations, a common practice in tribal societies, and even now, when everyone was facing destruction and exile, an old priest like Hanamel was not ready to forgo the ancient law.

At first, Jeremiah is puzzled by this request. Why would someone in jail, inside a city that is about to fall to the enemy, bother to buy a field he may never see? For what purpose? Moreover, he is old and childless. What would he do with this land?

And then Jeremiah begins to understand. This strange offer is a sign from God. Lately, he has started to doubt God's actions. Yes, destruction was imminent, inescapable. But redemption? How in the world will the exiles ever come back to this land? This has never happened before to any defeated and uprooted people. He must have misunderstood God's messages when God first told him years ago in that field in Anathoth in front of the blossoming almond tree that he was sending him to destroy and uproot, but also to build and to plant. Build and plant what, and where? Perhaps God had someone else in mind, not the people of Judah and Israel?

And suddenly it all becomes crystal clear. God has sent him a messenger in the person of his cousin, Hanamel. Ordinarily, Hanamel's request was a folly. Anyone who might have heard it would have laugh. But that was just the point. The buying of the field in Anathoth was not for the present, and certainly not for Jeremiah's own use. It was a solemn, symbolic act, an act of defiance. It was a statement. It said: Do not be afraid to buy a field in this land, for the day will soon come when the people who are now destroyed and exiled will return and, once again, buy fields, and till them, and sow them, and once again there will be joy and celebration in the fields of Judah and in the streets of Jerusalem.

Yes, Jeremiah says, I will buy the field:

> So I bought the field in Anathoth from my cousin Hanamel.
> I weighed out the money to him, seventeen shekels of silver.
> I wrote the deed and sealed it, and had it witnessed,
> and I weighed out the silver on a balance.
> I took the deed of purchase, both the sealed one containing the
> terms and conditions, and the open one. And I delivered
> the deed to Baruch the son of Neriah, son of Mahseiah,
> in the presence of my cousin Hanamel, and in the presence
> of the witnesses who were named in the deed,
> before all the Judeans who sat in the court of the guard.
> And I charged Baruch before them, saying, Thus says
> Adonai of hosts, the God of Israel: Take these deeds,
> this deed of purchase, both the sealed one and the open
> one, and put them in an earthen vessel, that they may last
> for many days. For thus says Adonai of hosts,
> the God of Israel: Houses and fields and vineyards shall
> yet again be bought in this land. (32:9-15)

Needless to say, the small crowd of detained people in the court of the guard watching this ceremony is hardly able to believe its eyes. The old man has surely lost his mind. But even they, somehow, are touched, and in their heart of hearts they begin to feel a stirring, a glimpse of what Jeremiah feels, of his unshakable faith in the future, and some of that faith begins to take hold of their own souls.

That night, Jeremiah is unable to sleep. He thinks of what he has done, and he feels an overwhelming need to talk to God. He feels the same way he did when God first spoke to him in his childhood. He finds himself saying the same thing he said to God back then: "Aha, God" (32:17)—a cry of bewilderment. His faith, on the one hand, is unshakable. But on the other hand, he is consumed with fear for the fate of his people. What will happen to them? People are dying every minute from battle wounds, from hunger, and from a cholera epidemic. And here you are, God, telling me to buy this field with silver in the presence of witnesses, while the city is about to fall to the enemy.

God replies, reminding Jeremiah that nothing is impossible for God. It is God's will that the enemy take the city and burn its houses, the roofs of which have been used for so long to make offerings to the Baal and to pour libations to other gods. But while the people may not be worthy of redemption, it is also God's will that they will in good time be gathered again from the lands of their dispersion and returned to their land, where God will replant them on their soil:

> I will rejoice over them to do them good,
> and I will plant them in this land in truth with
> My whole heart and with My whole soul.
> For thus says Adonai: Even as I have brought
> all this great evil upon this people,
> so will I bring upon them all the good
> that I have promised them.
> And fields shall be bought in this land
> Of which you say: It is desolate,
> without man or beast;
> it is given into the hand of the Babylonians.
> Men shall buy fields for money,
> and write the deeds, and seal them,
> and call witnesses, in the land of Benjamin,
> and in the places about Jerusalem,
> and in the cities of Judah,
> and in the cities of the hill-country,
> and in the cities of the Lowland,
> and in the cities of the South;
> for I will cause their captivity to return,
> says Adonai. (32:41-44)

23.

The Fall of Jerusalem

One by one, the towns around Jerusalem fall to the enemy. Finally, Jerusalem is left all alone. The pro-Egyptian party still hopes for a last-minute miracle. It is early summer, and the heat is intense. The stench of death is in the air. Food is running out. Water is scarce. The wailing of bereaved mothers can be heard in the streets. There are beggars everywhere. Old men sit on street corners looking up to heaven, waiting for a sign, but God seems to have long departed. The priests at the Temple no longer have sacrifices to offer. All they can do is pray in a faint voice, but there is no answer. The court prophets continue to promise a miracle, but their words sound hollow. Jeremiah's prophecy has come true. There is only one thing left to do—convince people that if they leave the city and turn themselves over to the Babylonians, their lives will be spared. If they stay, they will die.

Leaving the city is an act of treason, punishable by death. Word gets back to the king's officials about Jeremiah's seditious speeches. Three of them go to see the king:

> And Shephatiah the son of Mattan, and Gedaliah the son
> of Pashhur, and Jucal the son of Shelemiah, and Pashhur
> the son of Malchiah, heard the words that Jeremiah said
> to all the people, saying: Thus says Adonai: Whoever
> remains in this city shall die by the sword, by the famine,
> and by the pestilence; but he who goes forth to the
> Babylonians shall live, and his life shall be spared,
> and he shall live. Thus says Adonai: This city shall surely
> be given into the hands of the army of the king of Babylon,
> and he shall take it. Then the officials said to the king:
> Let this man, we pray you, be put to death; for as much as
> he weakens the hands of the men of war that remain in this
> city, and the hands of all the people, in speaking such words
> to them; for this man seeks not the welfare of this people,
> but their hurt. Then Zedekiah the king said: Behold, he is in
> your hands, for the king cannot oppose you in anything.
> (38:1-5)[17]

Once again, as has happened in the past, no one dares to kill Jeremiah. Instead, the king's officials decide to punish him in such a way that he may not come out alive.[18] They lower him with ropes into a deep pit where water was kept, but now only mud is left on the bottom. Jeremiah sinks into the mud, and is left there to die a slow death.

This should teach him a lesson once and for all, one of the officials tells his friend. This mud pit is where he belongs. Let God take care of him now.

His words are overheard by Ebedmelech, an Ethiopian slave of the king, a court eunuch. The slave goes to see the king, who is sitting at the Benjamin Gate, the gate where Jeremiah was first detained and where now a public hearing is taking place, during which people are free to bring their grievances to the court.

The slave falls down on his face before the king. The king orders him to stand up and state his business.

Pretending he does not know who had put Jeremiah in the mud pit, the slave says,

Some people must have put Jeremiah in the mud pit in the court of the guard. This is an evil thing, for he may be dead by now of starvation, since there is no food left in the city.

The king is startled. He realizes his officials had gone too far.

Go and gather thirty men, he orders his slave, and pull Jeremiah out of the pit before he dies.

The Ethiopian slave gathers the men. He takes some old clothes, and when they reach the pit he tells Jeremiah to put the clothes under his armpits, so that the ropes he is about to lower into the pit won't hurt him when he ties them around himself. Slowly, Jeremiah is pulled out of the pit. He is returned to his room in the court of the guard, where he will stay until Jerusalem falls.

The next day a messenger from the king arrives with orders to bring Jeremiah to the Temple. There, at the third entrance to the Temple, the king is waiting for him. The king orders his bodyguards to leave the two of them alone.

Jeremiah, the king says solicitously, I would like to ask you something, and I ask you that you tell me the truth.

I dare not tell you the truth, Jeremiah replies. If I tell you the truth you will put me to death. And if I give you advice, you will not listen to me.

Come closer, the king orders, so I can whisper in your ear.

Jeremiah draws closer.

So help me God, the king whispers, in the name of God who gives us life, I will not kill you or put you in the hands of these men who look to harm you.

Jeremiah raises his head and says in a solemn voice,

Thus says Adonai of hosts, the God of Israel, if you go out to the lords of Babylon you shall live, and this city will not be set on fire, and you and your household will live. But if you do not go out to the lords of Babylon this city will fall in the hands of the Chaldeans[19] who will set it on fire and you will not escape from them.

Zedekiah's face becomes grim.

I am afraid to turn myself over to them, for they will turn me over to the Jewish defectors who will torture me.

They will not turn you over to them. Listen to the words of Adonai that I am telling you and you will do well and you shall live. Otherwise, all the women of the king's palace will be taken out and given to men of the king of Babylon. All your wives and your sons will be taken, and you will not escape, and this city will burn down.

The king, looking down at the floor, remains silent for a long time. Finally, he lifts his eyes and says,

Jeremiah, tell no one what we spoke about. If my officials find out they will kill you. Tell them that you asked me not to return you to the house of Jonathan where you may die.

And here we are told that Jeremiah did exactly what the king told him to do. In other words, to save his life, he did not tell them the truth. As far as we can tell, this is the only time in his long prophetic career this man who was incapable of not telling the truth agreed to withhold the truth to save his life.

On the Ninth day of Av, the fourth month of the twelfth year of the reign of King Zedekiah, the walls of Jerusalem were breached. This date will become a day of fast and mourning for Jews for all time, during which the book of Lamentations, attributed to Jeremiah, is read in a special mournful chant. It is the moment the Jewish state is no more, and the future seems hopeless. We are told:

> In the ninth year of Zedekiah king of Judah,
> in the tenth month, came Nebuchadrezzar
> king of Babylon and all his army against Jerusalem,
> and besieged it; in the eleventh year of Zedekiah,
> in the fourth month, the ninth day of the month,
> a breach was made in the city—that all the officers
> of the king of Babylon came in and sat in the middle gate,
> even Nergal-sarezer, Samgar-nebo, Sarsechim Rab-saris,
> Nergal-sarezer Rab-mag, and the rest of the officers of
> the king of Babylon. (39:1-3)

From across the way, in the upper chamber of the palace, Zedekiah and his generals saw their enemies sitting in the middle of the city.

> When Zedekiah the king of Judah and all the men of war
> saw them, they fled, and went out of the city by night,

by the way of the king's garden, by the gate between the
two walls; and he escaped to Arabah. But the army of the
Chaldeans pursued them, and overtook Zedekiah in the
plains of Jericho; and when they had taken him, they
brought him up to Nebuchadnezzar king of Babylon to
Riblah in the land of Hamath, and they put them on trial.
Then the king of Babylon slew the sons of Zedekiah in
Riblah before his eyes; also the king of Babylon slew
all the nobles of Judah. And the eyes of Zedekiah were
put out and he was chained in bronze chains and brought
to Babylon. (39:4-7)

24.

After the Fall

Did Jeremiah cry when he saw the Holy Temple burn? As best we can tell, he did not. Forty-two years earlier, when he first received his prophetic charge, he knew that the Temple would be destroyed and he would live to see it happen. He had vivid visions of that terrible day. He saw and felt the suffering of his people, the long siege, the hunger driving people mad, forcing them to eat human flesh; the degradation of the royal family and of the temple priests and prophets; the looting of the holy of holies. Many a night he would wake up in a cold sweat and feel the pain in his gut. He began to mourn the coming destruction in his youth, and he kept mourning it all his life. Now that it finally happened, he had no tears left. He was kept in the court of the guard till the last moment, when the enemy entered the city. By now the guards were gone, and he was free to walk out and see it all. He felt numb with pain. His scribe, Baruch, was with him. The two of them walked silently as people around them gathered to turn themselves over to the invaders. It is too late, he said to himself, it is too late. Why didn't they turn themselves over when there was still time? What will happen to them now?

He wished he had never lived to see that day. But at the same time, he knew that God wanted him to live for a purpose. This was not the end—for him or for his people. This was a new beginning. God had made him see the future for a reason. He clearly remembered God's words,

> See, I have this day set you over the nations and
> over the kingdoms, to root out and to pull down,
> and to destroy and to overthrow; to build and to plant.
> (1:10)

To build and to plant. . . . Before long, the Babylonian empire will be no more. But these exiles will come back. They will rebuild this city, and they will plant the fields of Judah and Samaria once again.

Jeremiah is overcome with anger against the conquerors. He turns his eyes to the heavens and tells God:

> Pour out Your wrath upon the nations
> Who did not know You,
> And upon the families
> Who did not call Your name;
> For they have devoured Jacob,

They have devoured him and consumed him,
And have laid waste his habitation. (10:25)[20]

Clearly, the Babylonians had members of other nations with them, including neighbors of Judah, fighting against Jerusalem. Jeremiah, who for years predicted this terrible day, now feels unbearable bitterness in his throat. He reaches his arms up to heaven and, like Jacob wrestling with the angel of God, he wants to drag God off the heavenly throne and make the Almighty see the devastation. How could pagan nations defeat God's people? Slowly, his hands come down and he sinks into a reverie.

Jeremiah is awakened from his reverie by armed soldiers. He and Baruch are being chained together, and they see people all around them being chained and marched toward the Benjamin Gate, to begin their exile.

They are surprised their guards are not taunting them. Instead, they offer them water, and they order them to proceed through the gate.

After a while they reach Ramah, north of the city, not far from Jeremiah's native town of Anathoth. Jeremiah has a vision of Jacob's wife Rachel. He sees her standing by the wayside crying for her children who are being taken into captivity:[21]

A voice is heard in Ramah,
Wailing, bitter cry,
Rachel is mourning her children
Refusing to be consoled
For her children,
Now gone.

And God said:
Do not cry.
Do not shed tears.
For your labor will be rewarded.
For they will return from the enemy's land.
There is hope in your future,
Your children shall return to their border. (31:14-16)

There is Nebuzaradan, they hear someone say. He is the top man here. Nebuzaradan, the chief butcher, someone mumbles.

Jeremiah knows he has heard this name before. Nebuzaradan spots the man with the long white hair and flowing white beard. He walks over to Jeremiah.

Who are you? the Babylonian commander inquires.

I am Jeremiah, son of Hilkiah, from Anathoth.

Are you Jeremiah the prophet?

Yes, I am.

Are you the one who prophesied saying that God will bring evil on this place because you have sinned and did not listen to your God?

Yes, I did.

I have orders from the king to set you free. You are welcome to go with us to Babylon as a free person, or you can stay here or anywhere you like. And who is this man?

This is my scribe, Baruch the son of Neriah.

He is free to go too.

Nebuzaradan orders his men to remove Jeremiah's and Baruch's chains.

I have one question for you, Jeremiah. The king has ordered me to appoint a governor for the towns of Judah. Can you recommend anyone?

Yes, my lord. Gedaliah the son of Ahikam the son of Shaphan.

Very well. He is indeed our first choice.

My lord, I have one request of you.

Speak.

There is an Ethiopian slave of the king, Ebedmelech. He saved my life. Can I take him with me?

That same day Jeremiah, Baruch and Ebedmelech made use of their freedom and went to Anathoth, where Jeremiah reclaimed his estate.

25.

The Death of Gedaliah

The first thing Jeremiah probably does when he settles down in Anathoth is dictate to his scribe a lament for the fall of Jerusalem. He will continue to dictate those laments until the day he dies. They will form the basis for the book of Lamentations, the national cry of pain of the Jewish people to this day.

The new governor of the conquered province of Judah, Gedaliah son of Ahikam, takes residence in Mitzpah, north of Jerusalem in the land of Benjamin, not far from Anathoth. He invites Jeremiah to come and live in Mitzpah. His father, Ahikam, saved Jeremiah from the wrath of King Jehoiakim after the latter killed the prophet Uriah (26:24). His grandfather, Shaphan, was involved in the discovery of the scroll of the Torah in the days of King Josiah, along with Jeremiah's father, Hilkiah (II Kings 22:8-10). Quite clearly, Jeremiah was close to Gedaliah's family, which was viewed by the Babylonians as friendly and trustworthy, prompting them to appoint Gedaliah governor of the province. Thus the center of power shifts from Jerusalem, which now lies in ruins, to a place outside the land of Judah. Gedaliah is a man of peace, and to Jeremiah his appointment is a sign from God. Jeremiah believes Gedaliah was chosen to start the healing process and the reconstruction that would eventually lead to the return of the exiles, as Jeremiah had long prophesied.

Gedaliah's first task is to bring back as many of the people as he can who had fled to the neighboring countries of Moab, Edom and Ammon. He sends out messengers to let the refugees know they had nothing to fear, since the Babylonians were anxious to restore the land back to its normal state, so that they could derive benefits from this fertile province of their empire. There was much unclaimed land, much fruit to be gathered, vineyards to be harvested. Many people start coming back, and before long daily life is humming again, fields are harvested, the vineyards are yielding much wine, and the olive groves an abundance of oil. Jeremiah is heartened by what he sees. It seems that the hearts of the people may have begun to turn back to God, and before long the exiles in Babylon would start to come back.

But his hope is short-lived. There are still those who did not reconcile themselves to the renewed Babylonian yoke, and think they can carry on the fight to free Judah from the foreign invader. One of those people is a member of the royal seed named Ishmael son of Netaniah, who has saved his life by putting himself under the protection of Baalis, the king of Ammon. Ishmael is a cold-blooded opportunist who thinks he has a chance to be crowned king, and resents the appointment of Gedaliah as governor. The Ammonite king, who is no friend to Judah, arranges for Ishmael to assassinate Gedaliah as a way to bring strife among the Judeans and further weaken them, so he can expand his own borders.

Gedaliah is alerted by a former army officer named Johanan son of Kareah that Ishmael is rumored to be coming to kill him. But Gedaliah refuses to believe Johanan. To show that he is not afraid of Ishmael, he invites him to dinner at the governor's residence in Mitzpah. Ishmael arrives with ten of his men, all of them hiding daggers in their robes. During the dinner they suddenly rise and stab Gedaliah, killing him on the spot. They proceed to kill everyone in sight, including the Babylonian soldiers who were guarding the place.

The next day, before news of the massacre reaches the public, a group of eighty men from the towns of Samaria stop in Mitzpah on their way to Jerusalem where they are going to bring an offering to the House of God (which is now in ruins, and it is not clear whether the news of the fall of Temple have reached them). Ishmael invites them to see the governor, and when they reach the place he and his men start killing them and throwing their bodies into a common grave where the other dead are lying. When only ten of them are left, one of the pilgrims tells Ishamel they had gathered and hidden a large quantity of wheat and oil and honey, and if he spares their lives they would show him the place. Ishmael agrees to spare their lives in return for the ransom. He continues his orgy of killing and looting the town of Mitzpah, the new Babylonian seat of government, and returns to the safety of the land of Ammon, taking with him a large number of prisoners from Mitzpah.

> Johanan the son of Kareah and all the army officers
> that were with him heard of all the evil that Ishmael
> the son of Nethaniah had done. They took all their men
> and went to fight against Ishmael son of Nethaniah
> and found him by the great water source in Gibeon.
> When all the people held captive by Ishmael saw
> Johanan the son of Kareah and all the army officers that
> were with him they rejoiced. So all the people that
> Ishmael had carried away captive from Mitzpah cast about
> and returned, and went to Johanan the son of Kareah.
> But Ishmael the son of Nethaniah had escaped from
> Johanan with eight men, and went to the children
> of Ammon. (41:11-15)

What we learn from these stories, which are not told by Jeremiah but must have been originally inserted in the book by Baruch ben Neriah, is that the remnants of the people of Judah who were left in the land were not unified by a common cause. With the central government in Jerusalem gone, the people in the towns of Judah and Samaria were divided into factions headed by warlords who were being manipulated by neighboring rulers. Gedaliah was not up to the task of bringing those factions together, and he paid with his life.

The death of Gedaliah brings to an end any hope of continued sovereignty in the land of Israel. To this day, Jews mourn his death during the Days of Awe between Rosh Hashanah and Yom Kippur, as one of the most tragic events in their history.[22]

26.

Going Down to Egypt

We are not told how Jeremiah reacted to the murder of Gedaliah. We can only assume that he no longer hoped to see the restoration of Zion in his lifetime. It must have been clear to him that Jewish life in the conquered land would remain tenuous for a long time, and only long after he was gone would redemption begin. All he could do now was continue his literary work of providing written guidance for the future. For the rest of his days he will continue to dictate his prophecies to his scribe, and complete the work of gathering and writing the Torah.

Jeremiah wishes to remain in Anathoth where he hopes to die and be buried with his parents. But it is not meant to be. One day as he, Baruch, and Ebedmelech—the former slave to the king who is now assisting Baruch in taking care of Jeremiah—are taking a walk in the fields, a messenger from Johanan— the former army officer who gave chase to Ishmael and became the self-declared ruler of the land of Benjamin—arrives and tells them to pack their belongings and come along. It is no longer safe to stay in the land of Benjamin, as the Babylonians are coming to pacify the province, and many will die in the process. Jeremiah refuses to go, but he has no choice. The three of them are taken to a place near Bethlehem, south of Jerusalem, where Johanan and a large group of his followers, including entire families, are making preparations to go down to Egypt, where they hope to be done once and for all with the Babylonians, and begin a new life of safety and prosperity.

Baruch is vehemently opposed to going down to Egypt, and he makes his opinion known to the people around him. To him Egypt symbolizes slavery, going back to the pre-covenant days. He is afraid that everything he and Jeremiah have worked for will be lost. Jeremiah agrees. He has heard of the Jews living in Egypt, how they have brought with them many of the pagan practices he has fought against all his life. He never trusted the Egyptians, in whom he saw the historical enemy of his people. The last place he wants to go is Egypt.

It turns out they are not the only ones. Many people are having second thoughts about going to Egypt. There is a great deal of fear of the unknown. For several days they debate the issue and do not seem to come to an agreement. Finally they all agree to ask Jeremiah to consult God on this matter:

> Then all the army officers and Johanan the son of
> Kareah, and Jezaniah the son of Hoshaiah, and all
> the people from the least to the greatest, approached
> the prophet Jeremiah and said: Let our supplication,

we pray you, be acceptable to you, and pray for us to
Adonai your God, for all this remnant; for we are left
but a few of many, as your eyes can see us; that Adonai
your God may tell us which way we should go, and
what we should do.
Then Jeremiah the prophet said to them:
I have heard you and I will pray to Adonai your
God according to your words; and whatever Adonai
shall answer you I will let you know; I will keep nothing
back from you.
Then they said to Jeremiah: God be a true and faithful
witness for us if we do not do according to all the
words Adonai your God shall send you with to us.
Whether it be good, or whether it be evil, we will listen
to the voice of Adonai our God to whom we send you;
that it may be well with us when we listen to the voice
of Adonai our God. (42:1-6)

There is ambivalence in this exchange between the people and Jeremiah as to
the identity of God. When the people first address the prophet, they speak of
"Adonai *your* God" while Jeremiah speaks to them of "Adonai *your* God." Only
at the end do they refer to God as "*our* God." This ambiguity is at the heart of
Jeremiah's struggle to establish the universality of the one God. Clearly, Jeremiah
here is mocking them for referring to "his god" rather than the one God of all, and
finally they get the message and correct themselves.

Ten days later Jeremiah receives a message from God. He goes back to the
people and addresses them with a long exhortation designed to dissuade them
from fleeing to Egypt. He tries to reassure them God wants them to stay in Judah,
since God has promised not to bring destruction on them again. If they stay, they
will be blessed and good things will happen to them. On the other hand, if they go
to Egypt where they believe they "will not hear the trumpets of war and will not
starve" (42:14), the opposite will happen. The sword of Nebuchadnezzar will
reach them there, and they will die by the sword as well as of hunger and disease.
He reminds the people that they had come to him to ask for the word of God and
pledged to do as God commanded, and now they had to do what God is telling
them to do.

Once again, Jeremiah encounters disappointment:

Then spoke Azariah the son of Hoshaiah and Johanan
the son of Kareah, and all the proud men, and said to

> Jeremiah: You are lying. Adonai our God has not sent
> you to say: You shall not go into Egypt to live there;
> but Baruch the son of Neriah set you against us, to
> deliver us into the hand of the Chaldeans, that they may
> put us to death, and carry us away captives to Babylon.
> So Johanan the son of Kareah, and all the army officers
> and all the people did not listen to the voice of Adonai
> to dwell in the land of Judah. (43:1-4)

Jeremiah now understands that he is fated never to have the people listen to his words in his lifetime. Even now, when they have at long last recognized that he is a true prophet of God, they dismiss his words. Some day they will read those words and they will believe. But not now, not here:

> But Johanan the son of Kareah, and all the army
> officers took all the remnants of Judah
> who have returned from all the nations where
> they had been driven to dwell in the land of Judah,
> the men, and the women, and the children,
> and the king's daughters, and every person
> that Nebuzaradan the captain of the guard
> had left with Gedaliah the son of Ahikam
> the son of Shaphan, and Jeremiah the prophet,
> and Baruch the son of Neriah; and they came
> to the land of Egypt; for they did not listen
> to the voice of Adonai; and they came to
> Tahpanhes. (43:5-7)

27.

Jeremiah and the Legend of the Lost Ark

In the Second Book of Maccabees—an apocryphal book included in some Christian Bibles but not in the Jewish Bible—we find a legend according to which Jeremiah, on his way to Egypt, took with him the Holy Ark and arranged to have it buried at Mount Nebo on the east side of the Jordan where Moses had stood and looked at the Promised Land in the distance right before he died and was buried there. Jeremiah sealed the burial place of the ark so that it would not be found until such time when God gathered the people of Israel and brought them back to their land (II Maccabees 2:4-10).

We know that in the time of Jeremiah the kingdom of Judah was lost. We also know that the holiest object this kingdom possessed, namely, the Ark of the Covenant, had disappeared. According to the book of Exodus (25:10), the Ark was originally built during the Exodus to hold the two tablets Moses received from God upon which were inscribed the Ten Commandments. It was made of acacia wood, overlaid inside and out with gold. Each of its four corners had a gold ring for inserting on either side the two golden shafts used by the priests to carry the Ark. On top of the Ark, in the middle, was a seat, and at either end was a statuette of an angel or cherub spreading his or her wings forward over the seat. The presence of God was believed to dwell in that seat.

The Ark is mentioned over two hundred times in the Bible prior to the time of Jeremiah. It has several names, such as Ark of Adonai, Ark of the Covenant, Ark of the Testimony, the Holy Ark, and so on. Prior to the time of David it fell into the hands of the Philistines. It was restored to Israel, and the young David, who relocated the seat of his kingdom from Hebron to Jerusalem, brought it to his new capital city with great fanfare. Eventually, when his son, Solomon, completed the construction of the Holy Temple, the Ark was deposited in the most sacred chamber of the House of God, the Holy of Holies. As was mentioned before, when Solomon acceded to the throne, he banished Jeremiah's ancestor, the high priest Abiathar, who had conspired against him, to the priestly town of Anathoth, two to three miles northeast of Jerusalem, where Jeremiah would be born some three hundred years later. Solomon tells Abiathar that the reason he has decided to spare his life is because "You carried the Ark of Adonai our God before David my father, and you shared all his hardships." (I Kings 2:26)

The last time we hear about the Holy Ark is in the time of King Josiah, the king during whose reign Jeremiah began to prophesy. We read in II Chronicles 35:3:

> He [King Josiah] said to the Levites who taught all Israel,
> who were holy to Adonai, Put the Holy Ark in the house
> which Solomon the son of David king of Israel built;
> there shall no more be a burden on your shoulders:
> now serve Adonai your God, and his people Israel.

Without a doubt, during the time of the monarchy, which coincides with the period of the First Temple, the Ark is the holiest object the people of Israel possess. Jeremiah, no doubt, saw the Ark before it disappeared. As a member of a priestly family, quite possibly a family in charge of the care of the Ark, he was probably directly involved with attending to it. And yet, he remains silent as to the fate of the Ark at the time of the Babylonian conquest of Jerusalem. In fact, the Bible never mentions it again, as though it had never existed.

What ever happened to the Ark? Did the Babylonians carry it away along with the other booty they took from the Temple before they burned it down? Did the priests of the Temple hide it in the Temple Mount before the breach of the walls of Jerusalem took place? Was it removed from Jerusalem centuries later during the Crusades by Templar knights and carried off to Europe (France, Scotland and Ireland have been suggested)? Was it taken to Ethiopia? Or is the legend about Jeremiah taking upon himself the fate of the Ark true? We shall come back to this later on.

Jeremiah only mentions the Ark once, in the following verse:

> It shall come to pass, when you are multiplied
> and increased in the land, in those days,
> says Adonai, they shall say no more,
> The Ark of the Covenant of God;
> neither shall it come to mind;
> neither shall they remember it;
> neither shall they miss it;
> neither shall it be made any more. (3:16)

Although this prophecy appears early in his book, it may have been uttered after the Ark had disappeared. This statement is both harsh and unequivocal. The prophet is telling his people that in the future there will be no need for the Ark for, as he explains later on, after the exiles return from their captivity, God will enter upon a new covenant with His people and will inscribe the words of the covenant in their hearts. In saying "it shall be made no more," Jeremiah discourages the people from building a new Ark. He is signaling a transition in the religion of Israel—from a sanctified object of supernatural powers (as the Ark was believed to be), to the internalizing of the message contained in the object, namely, the Ten Commandments. What we have here is the beginning of a shift from a cultic religion, at the center of which stands the Holy Temple and its holy objects, to a religion at the center of which stands the house of assembly, prayer and learning, namely, the synagogue, in which the holy ark containing the scroll or scrolls of the Torah has replaced the original Ark of the Covenant to this day.

Jeremiah pronounces an unprecedented fivefold negation of the holiest object in Judaism:

> Will not be mentioned any more.
> Will not come to mind.
> Will not be remembered.
> Will not be missed.
> Will not be made any more.

We do not know whether Jeremiah spoke these words before or after the destruction of Jerusalem—in other words, while the Ark was still in the Temple, or after its disappearance. But in either case, he makes his position very clear: The holiest object in Judaism is only an object. For several centuries it was believed to be the object that bound the children of Israel to their God. It was believed to have divine powers. It contained the two stone tablets upon which God directly wrote the Ten Commandments "with the finger of God" (Exodus 31:18, Deuteronomy 9:10). God's presence, as a just and merciful God, dwelled upon it.

In light of all this, the above-quoted verse from the book of Jeremiah is, to say the least, quite extreme, and should be carefully considered. The first thing we learn from this quote is that indeed there was an Ark of the Covenant. While its divine powers are a matter of belief, its physical existence—considering the fact it is mentioned over two hundred times in the Bible over a period of centuries—is quite clear. But when we examine the legend in the Apocrypha in light of this verse, it is very hard to believe that Jeremiah bothered to take the Ark with him on his journey to Egypt. A far more likely possibility is that the Ark was hidden deep in the ground underneath the Temple by Temple priests rather than by Jeremiah, who was held prisoner at the time of the fall of the Temple. To those priests it was the most sacred object of their faith, the core of their being. Jeremiah, on the other hand, had come to the conclusion that devotion to holy objects is contrary to the spirit of pure monotheism, which is a belief in a non-material, transcendental power that exists apart from the physical universe human beings are part of. He realized that after the fall of Jerusalem the Ark becomes a thing of the past. His words, "Neither shall it be made any more," provide the clue that to

him it is a man-made object, not an object endowed with divine powers. He goes
on to say:

> At that time they shall call Jerusalem
> the throne of Adonai;
> and all the nations shall be gathered unto it,
> to the name of Adonai, to Jerusalem;
> neither shall they walk any more after the
> stubbornness of their evil heart. (3:17)

Here Jeremiah provides another clue as to why the Ark of the Covenant will
not be needed in the future: The Ark was setting Israel apart from the rest of
humanity. At the time of redemption (either in the near future when the exiles
return to the land or in the distant eschatological future), all humanity will believe
in the one God and there will be no need for God's presence to be limited to the
Holy Ark. The medieval Jewish Commentator Kimchi (RaDaK) has an interesting explanation: The Ark used to be carried to the battlefield to help win battles.
In the future, when peace is established and there is no longer a need to go to war,
there will be no longer a need for the Ark. Rashi adds that God's holiness will be
found throughout Jerusalem, not only in the Holy Ark.

Elsewhere in his book, Jeremiah explains why the Ark will become superflu-
ous:

> But this is the covenant that I will make with the
> house of Israel after those days, says Adonai,
> I will put My law in their innermost parts,
> and in their heart will I write it; and I will be their God,
> and they shall be My people; and they shall teach
> no more every man his neighbor,
> and every man his brother, saying:
> Know Adonai; for they shall all know Me,
> from the youngest to the oldest,
> says Adonai; for I will forgive their iniquity,
> and their sin will I remember no more.
> (31:32-33)

Jeremiah saw how the restoration of the Temple at the time of Josiah and the
presence of the Holy Ark in Temple's Holy of Holies did not bring about a change
of heart among his people. He was the first Hebrew who understood that if his
people were to truly embrace their faith they needed a new instrument to internal-

ize that faith—not two stone tablets inside an ark, but a scroll of the Torah that will be available to every Jew no matter where he lives, a *mikdash me'at*, a "small sanctuary" where every Jew—"from the youngest to the oldest"—can establish a personal relationship with God, learn the Torah, and live by its commandments. This vision of Jeremiah becomes the synagogue, the origins of which can be found in Babylonia during the exile. While the Temple will be rebuilt when the Exiles return from Babylonia (but will no longer house the Ark), it is the new institution called the House of Study and the House of Prayer, or synagogue, that will become the center of the Jewish faith. Inside that house there will be a holy ark containing the scroll of the Torah, the link between the Jew and God. This link has been the focus of Jewish worship and study for the past two thousand years, and will remain so long into the future.

28.

Prophecies to the Nations

When Jeremiah arrives in Egypt he encounters a Jewish community that has been living there since the first exile following the short reign of King Jehoiachin, twelve years earlier. He has known for some time this community was steeped in idol worshipping, particularly in the cult of the Queen of Heaven. When he comes face to face with this community and sees how far-gone it is in its idolatrous practices, and, in addition, he finds himself surrounded by the pantheon of Egyptian gods and goddesses and the huge monuments of Egypt, he wastes no time pronouncing prophecies against both Egypt and its new Jewish community. It is the same old Jeremiah who has not changed one bit over the years. He has not lost any of his eloquence and uncompromising bluntness. He meets his people and his new host country head-on and, once again, he is not making any friends or endearing himself to anyone.

We are not told much about his final years in Egypt, nor do we know how or where he dies. But it is more than likely that while in Egypt, with his scribe Baruch and his servant Ebedmelech, Jeremiah spent much of his time working on the Torah text and dictating prophecies for posterity. One thing becomes clear at this point: Jeremiah is the most thoroughgoing prophet since Moses. He does not leave one stone unturned in his zeal to fulfill his prophetic mission to Israel and to the world, namely, "to root out and to pull down, to destroy and to overthrow; to build, and to plant" (1:10). To achieve such a monumental task, he uses the media of the spoken and the written word. He engages in a major project of pronouncing prophecies not only over Israel, but also over all its neighbors, over the nations of his time that he is aware of, and particularly over the two empires of his time, Egypt and Babylon. One gets the impression that he firmly believes that if he puts a prophecy in writing, he ensures that its words, sooner or later, will come true. Seven years earlier, before the siege of Jerusalem, he wrote his prophecy against Babylon:

> The word which Jeremiah the prophet commanded
> Seraiah the son of Neriah, the son of Mahseiah,
> when he went with Zedekiah the king of Judah to
> Babylon in the fourth year of his reign. Now Seraiah
> was quartermaster. And Jeremiah wrote in one book
> all the evil that should come upon Babylon, all
> these words that are written concerning Babylon.
> And Jeremiah said to Seraiah: 'When you come to

Babylon, be sure to read all these words, and say:
O Adonai, you have spoken concerning this place,
to cut it off, that none shall dwell there, neither man
nor beast, but that it shall be desolate forever.
And when you finish reading this book, that you shall
bind a stone to it, and cast it into the midst of the
Euphrates; and you shall say: Thus shall Babylon sink,
and shall not rise again because of the evil
that I will bring upon her; and they shall be weary.
Thus far are the words of Jeremiah. (51:59-64)

Once in Egypt, Jeremiah has to decide where to turn his attention first—to the Egyptians or to his own people. He starts with the Egyptians. He invites "Jewish men" (here, in the Diaspora, we begin for the first time to hear the word "Jews," which originally meant people from Judah or Judeans) to come with him to the house of the Pharaoh in Tahpanhes, one of the towns where the Judean exiles have settled (44:1), when God commands him to

Take great stones in your hand, and hide them in
the mortar in the framework, which is at the entrance
of Pharaoh's house in Tahpanhes, in the sight of the
men of Judah; and say to them: Thus says Adonai of
hosts, the God of Israel: Behold, I will send and take
Nebuchadrezzar the king of Babylon, My servant,
and will set his throne upon these stones that I have
hidden; and he shall spread his royal pavilion over
them. And he shall come and smite the land of Egypt;
and those marked for death, to death, and those marked
for captivity, to captivity, and those marked for the
sword, to the sword. (43:9-11)

Jeremiah has now used stones, a multifaceted symbol of burden, destruction, and idolatry to seal the fate of both Babylon and Egypt. He now turns to the Judeans who live in Egypt and proceeds to chastise them with a long prophecy in which he describes in vivid detail the destruction of Judah and Jerusalem, and assures them that the same will happen to them if they do not mend their ways.

True to form, these people are no different from all their brothers and sisters whom Jeremiah has dealt with throughout his long prophetic career, never able to convince any of them to change their ways. They listen patiently to everything Jeremiah has to say, and when he finishes they tell him:

> Then all the men who knew that their wives offered to
> other gods, and all the women that stood by,
> a great assembly, even all the people that dwelt in
> the land of Egypt, in Pathros, answered Jeremiah,
> saying: for the word that you have spoken to us in
> the name of Adonai, we will not listen to you.
> But we will certainly perform every word that
> has come out of our mouth, to offer to the
> Queen of Heaven, and to pour out drink-offerings
> to her, as we have done, we and our fathers,
> our kings and our princes, in the cities of Judah,
> and in the streets of Jerusalem; for then we had
> plenty of food, and were well, and saw no evil.
> But since we ceased to offer to the Queen of
> Heaven, and to pour out drink-offerings to her,
> we have lacked all things, and have been consumed
> by the sword and by famine. (44:15-18)

It is quite remarkable that the traditional Jewish concept that appears in the Jewish prayer book, namely, "Because of our sins we were exiled from our land," has not yet taken root among these exiles. Quite to the contrary: These people believe that harm came to them because they stopped worshiping the female idol known as the Queen of Heaven (most likely as a result of Josiah's Reform), rather than their own God. To Jeremiah it becomes clear that these people are too far-gone, and he is convinced they will all perish. Whether or not that turns out to be the case, we do know that those exiles who did return to Judah less than a century later came from Babylon, not from Egypt.

Over the years, Jeremiah had pronounced many prophecies against the nations of his time. Now, having given up on his own people in the Egyptian exile, he begins to collect his prophecies to the nations, which become one of the sections of his book (chapters 46-51). In these prophecies no one is spared. He does not call upon the nations to repent. They have not entered into a covenant with the God of the universe, nor do they live by God's law. They are all temporal nations who have no staying powers. All of them live by the sword and are doomed to die by the sword.

Jeremiah is not the first prophet who prophesies against other nations, as he himself attests to:

> The prophets of old that have been before me and
> before you prophesied against many countries,

and against great kingdoms, of war, and of evil,
and of pestilence. (28:8)

But none of the prophets is more thorough in addressing every possible nation of the ancient Near East. Jeremiah's message is clear: there is only one power controlling the world. The destiny of great empires and of all people is in this power's hands. Moreover, the people of Israel had entered into a binding contract with that power, and they must live up to it. Otherwise, they can expect to be punished. Ultimately, however, in the fullness of time, this power will redeem them.

Like Moses before him, no one knows Jeremiah's burial place to this day.

Chapter Two

The Jewish and the Universal Jeremiah

1.

The Pivotal Prophet

Jeremiah lived through some of the most critical and turbulent events in history. It is a miracle that now, centuries later, explorers have been able to find such items dating back to that time as the Lachish letters, the seal impressions of personalities mentioned in his book, and more.[23] But perhaps the opposite is true. In very turbulent times things tend to be abandoned and lost, or even purposely hidden and buried for posterity. Witness the case of the Dead Sea Scrolls, dating to the time of the fall of the Second Temple, found hidden in desert caves; or items belonging to the Zealots dating back to the same time, found on top of the cliff overlooking the Dead Sea, known as Masada. The other miracle is that Jeremiah, who was never popular in his lifetime, lived to such a ripe old age and escaped death on several occasions. He lived long enough to play a role in Jewish and world history that made him what we might call the Bible's pivotal prophet. I am not suggesting that he should replace Moses as the key figure in Judaism. But in terms of our own human understanding of the nature of biblical prophecy, the relationship between the prophet and God, the message the biblical prophets sought to impart, and the implications of their teachings for our life today, the book of Jeremiah is a goldmine.

In Part One of this book we followed Jeremiah's career from the moment God called him to prophesy to the time when, exiled in Egypt after the destruction of Jerusalem, he disappears from the pages of history. The main source for this biographical inquiry is of course the book of Jeremiah itself. No other prophetic book in the Hebrew Bible provides more personal data or deals more intimately with the personal life and prophetic career of its namesake. And yet, the fifty-two chapters of the book are, for the most part, out of any chronological order; paragraphs and even verses within the same chapter often skip back and forth in time, and, in many cases, are very difficult to date. Moreover, it is clear that the book underwent several redactions, most likely by Jeremiah's scribe, Baruch ben Neriah, but also by later editors, whereby Jeremiah's original text is not always intact. Finally, the prophecies in the book are written in an impassioned poetic style that leaves room for various interpretations, and include some words whose meaning eludes us.[24] Consequently, much internal analysis as well as checking of other biblical texts and other historical and archeological sources had to be done, and such classical translations as the Septuagint (the 3rd century BCE Greek version of the Hebrew Bible), and a great body of biblical scholarship and commentaries—both classical and contemporary—had to be consulted in order to sort out the text written by and about Jeremiah in the book bearing his name and to create a cohesive interpretative portrait of the prophet.

No claim can be laid to total accuracy. There is a great deal we do not know, and can either take on faith or leave unanswered. But the overall picture of Jeremiah that emerges from this analysis points out to one conclusion: Jeremiah plays a pivotal role in the history of his people and their faith, and, consequently, in the history of monotheistic faith in general. Let us take a look at some of the lessons we learn from his life and teaching, and see how we can benefit from his timeless message.

2.

The Man Who Knew God

In the beginning of the book I made a rather bold remark about our prophet: Jeremiah knew God more personally and more intimately than perhaps even Moses. In the closing paragraph of Deuteronomy, which reports the death of Moses, we are told that the Father of the Prophets was closer to God than any other prophet: "There never arose another prophet in Israel whom God knew face to face" (34:10). Moses ben Maimon, or Maimonides, the greatest philosopher of Judaism, explains that the biblical Moses reached the highest rank of prophecy by communicating directly with God, while all the other prophets only heard voices or received signs or saw God in a vision or in a dream. Moses' career stretches over four biblical books—Exodus, Leviticus, Numbers and Deuteronomy. We have a wealth of information about his life, a life punctuated by some of the most awesome events in all of history—the plagues of Egypt, the crossing of the Red Sea, the giving of the law at Mount Sinai, and so on. And yet, one never gets the feeling Moses is someone you would meet on the street, shake hands with, or talk to. His monumentality is neither personal nor intimate. Quite possibly, layers of legend added to the real events of his life prevent us from really knowing Moses the person.

Moses' relationship with God is mostly one-sided. One does not detect any emotional involvement between the two. God commands and Moses obeys. We do not find Moses going through any uncertainty or questioning, except in rare instances. With Moses, everything seems to be preordained. God needed someone to free the Hebrew slaves and take them through the desert and give them the law, and Moses was chosen for the task.

Not so Jeremiah. As we become familiar with the torturous personal history of the prophet from Anathoth, we realize that from the moment God first becomes known to the young Jeremiah on a personal level, the relationship between the two is one of unusual intimacy, not found anywhere else in the Hebrew Bible. This intimacy causes Jeremiah to detach himself from his own family and his hometown, never marry or have children, limit himself to only one enduring friendship—the one with his scribe, Baruch, and live a solitary life. God fills his life to such a degree that there doesn't seem to be room for much else.

Jeremiah speaks to God on terms of intimacy:

> You are righteous, Adonai,
> But I will challenge You with words of judgment,

> Why do the wicked prosper,
> Why do the treacherous live in peace? (12:1)

Jeremiah probably knows the answer. God puts the righteous through trials. As for the wicked, they are always punished in the end, mainly by punishing themselves. But Jeremiah chooses to engage God in an intimate personal debate—indeed, "putting God on trial," because he hopes to convince God to find a better way to deal with humanity. Not only can people do better, God can also do better!

One may argue that it is the height of insolence (or *chutzpah*), to tell God what to do, better yet, put God on trial. God, however, does not strike Jeremiah dead. In fact, God protects Jeremiah throughout his long life and saves him from death several times. One of the most beloved figures in Jewish history, the eighteenth century Hasidic Rabbi Levi Yitzhak of Berdichev, was a latter-day reincarnation of Jeremiah. He used to talk to God on very familiar terms, and once he even summoned God to a *din torah*, a Jewish trial, putting God on trial for having dealt so harshly with His people Israel all throughout history. Levi Yitzhak, like Jeremiah, always concludes his complaint with an affirmation of his unshaken personal faith in God.

Elsewhere, Jeremiah says to God:

> You have seduced me,
> And I have been seduced. (20:7)

One cannot help but feel that every morning, when Jeremiah woke up, he said good morning to God. During the day he would hold conversations with God. And when he was in need of a prophecy, he prayed and pleaded and even cried, until he heard God speak to him. Sometimes he had to wait for several days for that voice to speak, as happened when the survivors of the fall of Jerusalem asked him to pray to God and find out whether they should go to Egypt, and he had to wait for ten days to hear God's answer. But whether or not he has to wait, God always speaks to him and tells him what to do.

The relationship between Jeremiah and God, in this author's opinion, is the basis for what Jewish and Christian theologians refers to as the personal relationship with God, reflected in the way Jews, Christians and Muslims speak to God either through their respective liturgies or in directly addressing God.

The concept of God as the cosmic father becomes palpable in the teachings of Jeremiah. Jews refer to God in their prayers as the heavenly father, or heavenly parent, *avinu she'bashamayim*. Rabbi Akiva, the second century sage and one of the greatest figures in Judaism, said:

Happy are you, O Israel,
For who purifies you,
And before whom are you purified?
Before your Heavenly Father. (Talmud Yoma 85b)

To Christians, God is "God the Father." This idea of the fatherhood of God, or, in a broader sense, the parenthood of God, is mainly attributable to Jeremiah, whose God says to the people of Israel:

Return, ye mischievous children,
And I will heal your mischief. (3:22)[25]

All throughout the book of Jeremiah, one gets the impression Jeremiah goes through life not only as God's emissary, or God's servant, but also—metaphorically speaking—as a son doing his father's bidding (in rabbinical literature—the Talmud and the Midrash—God is often compared to a king and man to the son of that king, as a way of explaining what God expects of people).

It must have been very difficult for Jeremiah to see his contemporaries not sharing his feelings towards God.[26] Their idolatrous practices and their superstitious belief in "gods of wood and stone" must have caused him great mental and physical pain. As he puts it: How can they turn away from the fountain of living water and build cisterns that can hold no water? How can a people who had been introduced to the true God centuries earlier embrace the useless religions of their neighbors? He spent his entire life trying to make them realize how wrong they were, and sought to bring them back to the "fountain of living water." And while he failed to achieve this goal in his own lifetime, after he was gone his people and later many other people began to benefit from the gift he gave the world—the intimacy between human beings and the one God.

3.

Jeremiah and the Nature of Prophecy

No other prophet in the Bible tells us so much about himself, his time, and the nature of biblical prophecy as Jeremiah. No other prophet bares his soul like this prophet, at once so human and vulnerable, yet hard as a rock and unwavering in his resolve. The time has come to give Jeremiah full credit for his unique accomplishments that are both particular and universal. Without him, Judaism may not have survived. Christianity and Islam may have never come into being. Human life as we know it would be entirely different. One may argue that, after all, Jeremiah is recognized as one of the greatest prophets in the Bible. This, however, is only half the truth. The other half is that he is the pivotal prophet in the Bible. Moreover, what we have here is a real person who lived and was in every way an important participant in the events of his place and time, and when we read his words and spend time deciphering his message, we realize that biblical prophecy is not about miracles, or the supernatural, It is a very human undertaking, reaching very deep into the human condition, relevant to its own time as well as to ours, indeed, universal and timeless.

Perhaps the most important thing we learn from the book of Jeremiah is that human beings are free to choose between right and wrong. Through nature, through their history, and through their common human experience, people receive messages as to what they need to do, but are always given the choice to accept or reject those messages. Many of Jeremiah's prophecies came true in his own lifetime, but that did not prevent his contemporaries from repeatedly rejecting his messages. We learn that human beings, whether ordinary people or people of great wisdom, wealth, and power have an extraordinary capacity to make mistakes and repeat them. People tend to imitate those around them, particularly those in power, and particularly those who do wrong, and they also tend to become creatures of habit, often time bad habits, and find it extremely difficult to change their ways. But at the same time, Jeremiah teaches us that human beings *can* change, for he never gives up hope for his people, no matter what. "Return, ye mischievous children," he calls out to them, "and I will heal your mischief" (3:22).

The next thing we learn is that it is quite often the fate of the prophet to be scorned and rejected. In the case of Jeremiah, it means a lifetime of rejection, a prophetic career of over forty years during which, from the very beginning to the very end the prophet's words fall upon deaf ears, even after he has become recognized as a true prophet. The biblical prophets were often scorned and mocked; they were called madmen, or even worse. Some, like Uriah the son of Shemaiah, were put to death; others, like Elijah, had to flee for their life; and others, like Jeremiah, suffered persecution, incarceration, physical torture, and were often a step from being put to death.

Moreover, what becomes quite clear in the case of Jeremiah and his contemporaries is that during the biblical prophetic period (which lasted for centuries) there was a constant debate over who is a true prophet. How can one tell a prophetic message from an idle figment of someone's imagination? When Jeremiah confronts Hananiah son of Azur, the prophet who breaks the yoke Jeremiah carries on his shoulders as a symbol of the inevitable rule of Babylon, Hananiah is introduced as a true prophet. And yet Jeremiah proves Hananiah's prophecy about the speedy delivery of Jerusalem to be false. During his entire career, Jeremiah has to contend with the court's prophets, who in reality are soothsayers for hire, doing the bidding of the king by dispensing false messages.

The struggle between true and false prophets in biblical times reaches its highest dramatic point with the ninth century BCE prophet Elijah and the four hundred and fifty false prophets of the Baal. In this story, Elijah, whose prophetic career coincides with the reign of King Ahab, decides to challenge the pagan prophets of the Baal and the Asherah, the two deities introduced into the kingdom of Israel by Ahab's Phoenician wife, Jezebel. He meets them at Mount Carmel, where an altar is prepared and a bullock is slaughtered and laid on the altar. Elijah challenges the pagan prophets to bring fire down from heaven to consume the sacrifice. They try for hours but are not able to do it, while Elijah addresses the crowd and asks the people to decide between Baal and the God of Israel. Finally, Elijah performs a miracle and brings down fire from heaven upon the altar.

Elijah belongs to the early generations of biblical prophets, known as nonliterary prophets because they did not leave any written records. Their stories were passed on orally, and were often embellished. When we reach the age of the literary prophets—the ones who have left written records, beginning with such prophets as Amos and Hosea, we no longer hear about prophets performing miracles. In the case of Jeremiah, his prophetic strength emanates from his personal conviction and his unswerving and consistent faith and vision. He may be trying to imitate predecessors like Elijah by dramatizing his messages with such props as a yoke of wood and a yoke of iron, or a soggy loincloth, or an earthen bottle, but none of it amounts to a miracle. It is the message that matters, not the drama.

Perhaps the most common and the most significant characteristic of the biblical prophets is their total and extreme devotion to what they perceive as the divine truth, and none of them is more consistent than Jeremiah. Living through the most harrowing and tragic period in biblical history, he never chooses to water down his message because of external or expedient circumstances. He may be flogged, he may be thrown into the mud pit, or he may be witnessing Jerusalem burning, but none of this will stop him from telling the truth, from speaking truth to power, from challenging the complacency and the short-sightedness of his people. This absolute adherence to the truth, as was pointed out by the Hebrew thinker Ahad Ha'am in his essay *Priest and Prophet*, is the hallmark of the prophet. God does not speak in nuances the way people do. With God right is an absolute right, and wrong is an absolute wrong. When kings like David or Ahab commit a crime against one of their subjects, prophets like Nathan and Elijah condemn them in dire terms. One misdeed against a single subject amounts to a total failure to live up to what God expects of the divinely anointed king. When Jeremiah sees a Jerusalemite cheating his neighbor or burning incense to the Queen of Heaven, he realizes that the renewal of the covenant between God and Israel under the auspices of King Josiah has failed. To him, a just society living by the laws of the covenant does not condone any act of immorality or idolatry by any individual member of society.

It is important to keep in mind that despite the prophetic adherence to absolute truth, Jeremiah, like the rest of the prophets, is only human. He is not a divine being. Being human, he has his doubts and his fears. He is not always sure of his received prophetic message. He is often questioning himself, agonizing over his mission. The burden he is carrying is enormous. He realizes this from the moment when, as a child, God first speaks to him. He is not a self-assured, strong-minded soldier in the service of God. Between prophecies, he is a humble person, very sensitive and vulnerable. The moment he has to confront his people and speak the word of God, the word will come out—to borrow the metaphor of Saadia Gaon, the tenth century Jewish philosopher—like the blast of the ram's horn, loud and deafening. At that moment it is not Jeremiah the man speaking, it is the word of God. At that moment he is fearless, like a lion ready to pounce on its prey. At that moment, it seems, he becomes more than himself.

The biblical prophets were a unique phenomenon in the cultural and spiritual history of the world. They served as a model to the founders of other monotheistic religions, and they continue to inspire all those who speak out and fight for human rights, justice, and integrity, everything that makes human life human. They cared for the weakest members of society—the widow and the orphan, the poor and the elderly. They cared for the strangers in the midst of their people, "For ye were strangers in the land of Egypt." And they cared for the slave, be it a Hebrew slave, who had to be set free on the seventh year, or the Ethiopian slave, Ebedmelech, who saves Jeremiah from the mud pit. Their moral vision has no parallel in history. To compare them to the oracle of Delphi in ancient Greece is to insult them, for they were not soothsayers. To compare them to the Greek philosophers is to diminish them, for although people like Socrates made a singular contribution to human wisdom and showed great integrity, and although Socrates was willing to die for what he believed in, neither he nor any other philosopher that ever lived can lay claim to what is perhaps the greatest insight the human race has ever had, namely, that there is one God in the universe; that this God is personal and cares about every human being; that all people, no matter how humble or powerful are children of the one God; and that divine justice is not conditional or relative, but rather absolute and inescapable. This is the message the biblical prophets have given the world in the pages of the Hebrew Bible, a message much of the world has sought to live by during the past twenty centuries, a message as valid today as it was 2600 hundred years ago, when a man from the town of Anathoth north of Jerusalem first spoke out against the failings of his people.

Jeremiah, however, unlike the other Hebrew prophets, is not only a prophet of divine justice. He is also a prophet of divine love. Polemics between Christianity and Judaism have often revolved around the proposition that in Christianity love becomes a higher value or a greater power than justice. On the Jewish side of the argument, the point has always been made that love is a relative and conditional aspect of human life, which cannot be relied on in every instance, while justice is the only way to ensure that good is rewarded and evil is punished. The Christian response has been that love can heal, redeem and so on, hence it is superior to justice. Actual human experience, however, shows that both justice and love are necessary for human welfare. In Jeremiah, both live side by side. For a prophet who chastises his people more harshly and more relentlessly than any other prophet, he also has the most tender and loving words for his people of any other prophet. His first prophecy begins with the words:

> I remember the devotion of your youth,
> The love of your betrothal. (2:2)

When his people go into exile he can hear the matriarch of Israel cry:

> Rachel is crying for her children,
> Refusing to be consoled. (31:14)

When his people feel that God has abandoned them, he reassures them with the words:

> How dear to Me is my son Ephraim,
> The child in whom I delight. (31:19)

And his love is not limited to his own people. His last act before going into exile is saving the Ethiopian slave Ebedmelech, whom in all likelihood he took with him to Egypt (39:16-18). In short, in the historical debate between Judaism and Christianity as to whether love is more important than justice, Jeremiah's answer appears to be that both are equally important.

4.

Jeremiah and the Other Prophets

What is a prophet? In every human culture since the beginning of time there were individuals who laid claim to special powers that permitted them to predict the future. This gift of divination manifested itself in many different ways and employed many different methods. In some cultures, one had to go into a trance to receive a vision or a message. In others, one remained lucid and calm and studied such natural phenomena as the flight of birds or the weather patterns, or even resorted to using tea leaves or coffee grounds. One could make a good case that what those future-tellers were really doing was use their common sense and experience rather than the method that was popular in a particular place and time. No doubt, prophecy among the ancient Hebrews was practiced in similar ways, and such practices continued until the end of the biblical period. The people who pursued such methods are referred to in the Bible as false prophets. But then something happened that was entirely different from anything known until that point: this small people named Israel, surrounded by great empires and well developed civilizations, gave birth to a new breed of prophets referred to by the Bible as true prophets. Along with this new breed of prophets a new radical idea came into the world: all other prophets—whether among the Hebrews or among the nations—were false. In an act of supreme defiance against all the established cultures and religions of the time, this people came to the conclusion that all the other so-called prophets were not really prophets, but rather people engaged in acts of pretense and make-believe. The Hebrew prophets hammer at this point over and over again: pagan prophets are not prophets, since pagan religions are devoid of any meaning, while Hebrew prophets are not prophets simply because they say they are. Somehow, one has to prove oneself to be a prophet. How exactly, is not always clear.[27]

Beginning with Moses, the Hebrew prophet was expected to have the ability to perform miracles. In fact, Moses' preeminence as a prophet was predicated on his ability to perform miracles of such magnitude that no other prophet after him was ever able to come even close. Interestingly, post-biblical Judaism tried to explain why Moses was able to defy the laws of nature as in the case of splitting the Red Sea while no such thing ever happens again by arguing that when God created the world, "God mandated" that the sea would split at that particular point in time.[28] In other cultures, stories of miracles are commonplace. In Christianity, the performance of miracles is attributed to saints. In post-biblical Judaism, it appears in folk traditions, sometimes associated with Jewish mysticism and, in the last three centuries, with Hasidic rabbis. Early biblical prophecy continued to attribute to the prophet the ability to perform miracles, as we saw in the story of Elijah and the false prophets of the Baal. But as we reach the time of the literary prophets, namely, the ones who have left a written record of their prophecies, miracles are no longer the prophetic method of choice. At this point Hebrew prophecy reaches an entirely new level, in which the prophet focuses on the adherence to the belief in the one God of the universe, complete renunciation of pagan practices, and an uncompromising commitment to a moral code of social behavior. The theological and ethical focus of these prophets is what they stake their authority on, and it is summarized in the Ten Commandments.

This peerless breed known as the literary Hebrew prophets is the greatest contribution Judaism has made to the world. For Jews, the literary prophets to this day are the spokespersons of God, and their words continue to instruct and inspire. To Christians, the prophetic prototype and the prophetic message provide the model and the underlying ideology for the founder of Christianity. For Muslims, they provide the model for the founder of Islam and his teachings. More recent variations of Christianity, such as the Mormons, also follow a prototype of their own prophet/founder, as do later variations of Islam, such as Baha'ism. Without the prophetic model, monotheistic civilization as we know it is inconceivable.

Unlike Christianity and Islam, who limit the concept of a prophet to one person, namely, their founder or originator, in ancient Israel there were many who claimed to be prophets. The first king of Israel, Saul, anointed by the prophet Samuel, makes an attempt to prophesy, and is mocked by his contemporaries ("Is Saul also a prophet?" people ask one another, which leads us to conclude that it was not an uncommon practice at that time to try to prophesy [I Samuel, 10:11]). In the time of Elijah, during the early stages of biblical prophecy, we hear of entire schools of prophets and of groups known as *b'nai nevi'im,* sons or disciples of prophets (II Kings 2:15).

How did one become recognized as a prophet? We can ask the same question in regard to artists. How does one become recognized as a Shakespeare or a Beethoven? By the cumulative acceptance of the artist's work over time. Certain prophets received this cumulative acceptance and were included in the biblical canon. No doubt, there must have been others whose words also deserved to be included in the canon but might have been lost. Others, who did find their way into the Bible, are represented by a few fragments of their work. Altogether, only fifteen prophets have their own biblical book, beginning with the three known as the "major prophets," namely, Isaiah,[29] Jeremiah and Ezekiel, followed by the twelve "minor prophets," namely, Hosea, Joel, Amos, Obadiah, Jonah, Micah, Nahum, Habakuk, Zephaniah, Hagai, Zechariah, and Malachi. The terms "major" and "minor" refer to the size of a particular book, not to the relative importance of each particular prophet.

Jeremiah shares certain key ideas with some of the other prophets, and even borrows from some of his predecessors. The main idea Jeremiah focuses on is the one enunciated in the first of the Ten Commandments, namely, "I am Adonai your God." Everything else flows from this idea. Conversely, idolatry is the worst transgression of all, for it denies the omnipotence of God. This idea, according to Jeremiah and his predecessors, leads to the next idea, which is obedience to God, or doing God's will. What is God's will? The most striking answer to this question is given by the prophet Micah: "It has been told you, O man, what is good, and what Adonai requires of you, but to do justice, and love mercy, and walk humbly with Adonai your God (6:8). The prophet Samuel, predating Micah, asks rhetorically: "Does God crave burnt offerings and sacrifices, or obeying the word of God?" (I Samuel 15:22). To Jeremiah, the moral law takes precedence over the ritual law. The only validity the ritual law has is when it follows and complements ethical behavior. Sacrifices without morals are useless, a point he begins to make early in his career and adheres to until his dying day. Like his predecessors, Jeremiah is the champion of the weak and the oppressed who are the perennial testing ground of ethical behavior. Finally, like all his predecessors, Jeremiah believes that evil, both personal and collective, does not go unpunished. God sees and remembers, and at the appropriate moment God calls the evildoers to account.

It has been argued that the Hebrew prophets were opposed to the sacrificial cult of their time, practiced by the priestly class, and sought to establish a new religious practice based on faith and ethics. This is not entirely true, since at no time do the prophets call for the abolition of the temple cult. Jeremiah and, even more so, his younger contemporary, Ezekiel, envision the future restoration of the temple cult. Being a product of their time, they cannot conceive of worshipping the God of Israel without this cult. When Isaiah has his vision of the end of days, he puts at the center of his vision the Temple in Jerusalem, and sees many nations flocking to that temple to hear the word of the one God. In post-biblical Jewish tradition, the belief in the messianic age is built around the restoration of the Temple. But in actual historical fact, once the Temple is destroyed by the Romans in 70 CE, the sacrificial cult ceases to exist in Judaism, although remnants of it linger, as in the case of the Samaritans in today's West Bank who sacrifice a lamb on Passover.

To Jeremiah, the two key prophets in Jewish history are Moses and Samuel (15:1). Moses is the liberator and lawgiver. His preeminence as liberator and lawgiver is never questioned. The Torah and Moses are synonymous. Under Moses, the tribes of Israel become the people of Israel and enter into the covenant with God. This, to Jeremiah and his colleagues, is the central event of history. The next key figure in prophetic history is Samuel. Three hundred years after Moses, the tribes of Israel are still divided among themselves and vacillate about adhering to their monotheistic faith. It takes the leadership of a Samuel, who is a judge as well as a priest and a prophet, to rally the tribes and establish the monarchy as one faith community, culminating in the anointing of the young David, who becomes the king of Israel par excellence and eventually the messianic prototype. Jeremiah sees Moses and Samuel as his models. He realizes that he is living in an age when his people once again, as happened before in the time of those two other prophets, have reached a point of profound crisis, and it is his mission to help them out of this crisis and move them on to the next stage of their history.

But Moses and Samuel are not his only two models. As a young man on the threshold of his prophetic career, Jeremiah comes under the influence of a female prophet known as Huldah, whose prophecy about the fall of the kingdom of Judah becomes his own core prophecy. Unlike Moses and Samuel, about whom we know a great deal, Huldah is only mentioned once, and it appears as though the only reason she is mentioned is to set the stage for Jeremiah.

Another prophet who influences Jeremiah both in style and in substance is Hosea, who precedes him by about a hundred years. Hosea lived in the Northern Kingdom (Israel) shortly before it was destroyed by Assyria (in 721 BCE). He sees the people of the Northern Kingdom as a wife that has betrayed her husband. To dramatize his view, he marries a prostitute who bears him children whom he gives such names as to dramatize the way Israel betrayed her God. Hosea then goes on to predict that in the future Judah and Israel, having turned away from their sins, will come together and will renew their covenant with God, which he compares to a marriage. Here he pronounces words that affirm the eternal nature of the covenant between God and Israel:

> And I will betroth you forever,
> And I will betroth you with justice
> And righteousness and kindness and mercy,
> And I will betroth you with faithfulness
> And you will know Adonai. (Hosea 2:21-22)

One can hear Jeremiah's first prophecy, "I remember the love of your betrothal" echoed in these words, as though he picked up where Hosea left off. The motif of a marriage between God and Israel is clearly borrowed from Hosea. We have discussed this motif in a special chapter dealing with the question why Jeremiah seems to be so obsessed with the idea of marriage between God and Israel.

5.

Jeremiah's Disciple

The prophets most influenced by Jeremiah are Ezekiel and the Second Isaiah. Ezekiel is practically a contemporary of Jeremiah, though some years younger. He is sent to Babylon with the first exile in the time of King Jehoiachin. What is remarkable about the book of Ezekiel is that within a short time of living in the Babylonian exile, Ezekiel develops a Hebrew style and coins new words unknown to Jeremiah, most likely influenced by the language or languages spoken in Mesopotamia.[30] He also uses innovative Hebrew terms, such as *ben-adam*, or son of man, which he keeps repeating. But despite the linguistic differences, Ezekiel spreads among the Babylonian exiles the message that for years now has been delivered by his older colleague back home in Jerusalem.

The first example of this ideological kinship between Jeremiah and Ezekiel is the way the latter dwells on the female image of Israel and Judah as two sisters who prostitute themselves with all the neighboring nations and with world powers such as Egypt and Assyria. Here Ezekiel appears to develop a theme started by Jeremiah concerning Judah's betrayal of her God. (Ezekiel 23)

The second example is Ezekiel's concern with the ancient biblical belief that the sins of the fathers are visited upon their sons. When the Judeans are first exiled to Babylon, the common belief among them is that they were punished for the sins of their predecessors, particularly the ones who lived during the reign of King Menasseh, who for fifty-five years did "that which was evil in the eyes of God." Having lived under the reigns of Josiah and Jehoiachin, following the great religious reform, they did not consider themselves sinful enough to have deserved exile. The idea of people paying for the sins of their fathers was deeply ingrained among the ancient Hebrews, as it was among neighboring nations. In his prophecy concerning the future redemption of Israel, Jeremiah states:

> In those days they shall no longer say: The fathers have
> eaten sour grapes and the children's teeth are blunted.
> Everyone shall die for his own sins; every person that
> eats the sour grapes his teeth shall be blunted.
> (31:29-30)

Here Jeremiah lays the groundwork for individual responsibility. The significance of this concept, which breaks with centuries of tradition, is enormous. Until now, the members of the Hebrew tribes have seen themselves as part of a group rather than as individual persons. The implication was that if a member of the tribe sinned, his action resulted in collective punishment. Jeremiah is looking

into the future and sees a new era in which the sins of the fathers will not be
visited on their children. Each person will be personally accountable for his or
her own deeds. In tossing this idea into the world, Jeremiah is beginning the
process of transitioning his people—as we discussed earlier—from "Hebrews"
to "Jews." In other words, from tribal people to people whose relationship with
God is direct and personal, and who can take individual responsibility for their
actions and become accountable for them strictly on their own.

Ezekiel takes this idea a step further. In one of the most remarkable passages
in the entire Bible, he provides his own novel understanding of this concept.
Here, more than anywhere else in his book, his role as Jeremiah's spiritual heir
becomes clear. Moreover, there is a clear indication here that Jeremiah's prophecies were transmitted to the new exiled community in Babylon, probably as early
as the time of Jehoiachin's exile, namely, during Jeremiah's own lifetime. What
this means is that while the Judeans did not listen to Jeremiah, members of the
early Babylonian exile did begin to listen to him, most important among them
Ezekiel:

> The word of Adonai came unto me, saying:
> What do you mean that you speak this proverb
> in the land of Israel, saying:
> The fathers have eaten sour grapes,
> and the children's teeth are blunted?
> As I live, says Adonai, you shall not have
> occasion any more to use this proverb in Israel.
> All souls are Mine; the soul of the father
> and the soul of the son are Mine;
> the soul that sins, it shall die.   (18:1-4)

Here Ezekiel, the prophet of the exile, is reacting to what the people back
home in Judea are saying about the reason for the exile: their ancestors sinned
and they are being punished. He reaffirms Jeremiah's prophecy, which is also a
reaction to this belief. More significantly, unlike Jeremiah who speaks about a
time to come, Ezekiel is taking the idea of individual responsibility a giant step
further by stating that it goes into effect here and now. The process of national or
collective punishment has ended. From now on the tribal concept is being replaced by the concept of individual responsibility. From now on each Jew is directly responsible to God for his or her own actions, since God is the God of all
souls (Jews as well as non-Jews) rather than a national God.

6.

The Second Isaiah and Jeremiah

A generation or two after Ezekiel, one or more prophets arose, most likely among the Babylonian exiles. We have absolutely no biographical data about those particular prophets. Their prophecies were attached to the book of Isaiah, who lived almost two centuries earlier. Why this was done no one seems to know. One could only guess that the reason for it was that the prophet in question—or the dominant prophet in the group—was also called Isaiah. These prophecies begin with chapter 40 of the book of Isaiah. Major Jewish biblical scholars such as Yehezkel Kaufmann only recognize one such prophet, named the Second Isaiah, while some scholars believe there was a Third Isaiah or perhaps even more.[31] Be this as it may, this mysterious post-Jeremiah prophet, the Second Isaiah, is without a doubt one of the most influential prophets of the Hebrew Bible. He seems to take the prophecies of his predecessors, such as Amos, Hosea, the First Isaiah and particularly Jeremiah, to a higher level. His impact on both Judaism and Christianity has been enormous. Furthermore, his impact on Christianity in particular has been crucial. Christian scholars of all the many varieties of Christianity have been focused on one particular text in the Second Isaiah known as the "suffering servant" text, as an Old Testament prophetic proof of the life and martyrdom of the Christian messiah:[32]

> Who can believe what we have heard?
> And on whom was Adonai's power revealed?
> He rose like a child before Him
> And like a tree trunk in an arid land;
> He had no rank and was given no respect,
> We did not find anything attractive about him.
> He was despised, shunned by all,
> A great sufferer, greatly afflicted,
> He seemed to hide from us,
> Despised, we took no account of him.
> Indeed, he carried our affliction,
> And he suffered our pain,
> And we thought him diseased,
> God stricken, tortured.
> But he was stricken
> Because of our sins,
> Oppressed because of our iniquities,
> The lesson of our welfare is upon him,

> And in his bruises we were healed.
> We all went astray like sheep,
> Each going our own way,
> And upon him God visited the guilt of us all.
> He was attacked, yet he remained submissive,
> He did not open his mouth.
> He was led like a sheep to the slaughter,
> Silent as a ewe about to be sheared.   (53:1-7)

Anyone who has carefully read the previous chapters of this book can readily see who it is the Second Isaiah is talking about. Nevertheless, for centuries, Jewish and non-Jewish scholars have differed vigorously on who the "suffering servant" of God was. To Jews, it has been the Second Isaiah himself and, by extension, the people of Israel, whom God sorely afflicted because of their failure to keep the covenant and be a "light to the nations," thus making an example of them to the rest of the world. To Christians, it was the Christian messiah, foreshadowed in these prophetic words. In fact, Christian teachers have clutched this passage so tightly to their bosoms, that many people must think it is part of the New, rather than the Old Testament.

Both appear to be wrong. The Second Isaiah speaks of a specific person, and for some undisclosed reason he does not give out his name. One possible explanation is this: he is prophesying during the time of the Babylonian Exile and the return to Zion. It is the time when the primacy of Moses ("the man of god") is being established as the Jews transition from Temple-centered to Torah-centered Judaism, and he does not want to elevate this person to the rank of Moses. However, he does recognize the critical role of this person in enabling the Jewish people to survive exile and return to their land.

As for the Christian theory about the foreshadowing of the gentle man from Galilee, let us hear what a contemporary Christian scholar has to say:

> So Isaiah sketches his portrait of the coming Servant of the Lord
> who should save Israel, and in that portrait Jesus himself saw his
> own lineaments and destiny prefigured. But of whom was
> Isaiah thinking when he asked his questions? With Jeremiah's
> story in mind, we may reverently wonder if the words do
> not describe his experience with astonishing accuracy.
> And reverent surmise becomes moral certainty when we hear
> Isaiah at once quote Jeremiah's words about himself: "But I
> was like a gentle lamb led to the slaughter. I did not know it

was against me they devised schemes, saying, . . . 'Let us cut
him off from the land of the living.'" (Jer. 11:19; cf. Isa. 53:7-8)[33]

This quote from the Reverend R.E.O. White, an ordained Baptist minister, is about the most honest and accurate commentary on the topic of the "suffering servant" I have ever come across. I find him to be correct on both scores: (a) the unnamed person is the prophet Jeremiah, and (b) Jeremiah served as a role model for Jesus.

Let us look at each verse and find out how it applies to Jeremiah:

"Who can believe what we have heard?
And on whom was Adonai's power revealed?"

The story of Jeremiah is absolutely amazing. For a while it was unknown in Babylon, but when the Second Isaiah first heard it he was amazed to learn what Jeremiah had gone through, and how God chose such an afflicted person as his messenger.

"He rose like a child before Him
And like a root in an arid land"[34]

Here we have God first revealing Himself to the child Jeremiah, as Jeremiah hears God's voice for the first time in the blossoming almond tree.

"He had no rank and was given no respect,
We did not find anything attractive about him."

Jeremiah gave up his priestly title. He was not an official prophet of the court until the very end, when King Zedekiah treats him as one without actually bestowing the rank on him. Jeremiah's contemporaries are never attracted to him.

"He was despised, shunned by all,
A great sufferer, greatly afflicted,"

Jeremiah was the most afflicted prophet in the Hebrew Bible. Indeed, a great sufferer, shunned by all.

"He seemed to hide from us,
Despised, we took no account of him."

Hiding is a theme in Jeremiah's life. After he prophesies at the Temple, the priests try to put him to death, and he is banned from appearing in public and seems to be hiding. Later, after King Jehoiakim throws his scroll of prophecies into the fire, he has to go into hiding to save his life.

"Indeed, he carried our affliction,
And he suffered our pain"

No other prophet in the Bible suffers the pain of his people more than Jeremiah. He begins to suffer the horrors of the destruction of Jerusalem long before they actually happen.

And we thought him diseased,
God stricken, tortured.

Many in Jerusalem must have thought of Jeremiah as an afflicted person, often engaged in odd behavior, as in the story of the wet loincloth. Many might have regarded him as someone being punished by God.

"But he was stricken
Because of our sins,"

God indeed makes Jeremiah carry the burden of the sins of his generation.

"Oppressed because of our iniquities,
The lesson of our welfare is upon him,"

The life of Jeremiah and his teaching were an object lesson for his generation. That they recovered their national welfare was because of him and the legacy he bequeathed them, namely the Torah and prophetic teachings he preserved for them with the help of his scribe, Baruch ben Neriah. More specifically, Jeremiah in his letter to the Babylonian exiles tells them to pray for the welfare of their city of exile, whereby they were able to endure years of exile and eventually return to their land.

"And in his bruises we were healed.
We all went astray like sheep,"

When Jeremiah is flogged, or when he is lowered into the mud pit, he emerges full of bruises. But he is doing it for the sake of his people, all of whom went astray and did not see the impending doom.

> *"Each going our own way,*
> *And God visited upon him the guilt of us all."*

The people were divided during the time of the siege of Jerusalem, and Jeremiah had to live through that time of national divisiveness and bear its consequences (especially during the assassination of Gedaliah, the governor appointed by the Babylonians after the fall of Jerusalem). Jeremiah suffered the consequences of the conflicts among his people to the very end.

> *"He was attacked, yet he remained submissive,*
> *He did not open his mouth."*

When the priests at the Holy Temple try to pass a death sentence on Jeremiah, he humbly accepts his fate, and is only saved by the intercession of a high-placed friend.

> *"He was led like a sheep to the slaughter,*
> *Silent like a ewe about to be sheared."*

Here we have Jeremiah's own words being quoted: "But I was like a gentle sheep led to the slaughter" (11:19).

We should keep in mind that The Second Isaiah addresses the descendants of the exiles who have recently returned from Babylon and from other parts of the new Persian Empire. What this prophet seems to imply in these verses is that Jeremiah played the central role in the redemption following the destruction of the First Temple. That he does not mention Jeremiah by name should come as no surprise, considering the fact that he does not mention any of his contemporaries by name, not even himself (unlike Jeremiah, who mentions many of his contemporaries by name). As was mentioned before, at that time, the time of the return from Babylonian exile, the returning exiles were focused on the antiquity and authority of the Torah of "Moses the man of God" which was now becoming the centerpiece of their faith, and by necessity played down the role of Jeremiah, who represented recent history.

That the Second Isaiah meant to foreshadow the career of Jesus by describing the life of Jeremiah is a matter of belief, not of historical fact. The more accurate assessment, as the Reverend White has indicated, is that Jesus himself modeled his life after the life of Jeremiah. Reading the Gospels as a Jew, I cannot help but be amazed at the way Jesus keeps predicting everything that is about to happen to him, step by step, day by day, as he does, for example, in the story of

the last supper and its aftermath. Here was a man of rare qualities, who took his
destiny in his own hands and played it out as a role model for future generations,
much the way Jeremiah did. The Reverend White goes on to say:

> Not only did some men say that Jesus *was* Jeremiah
> (Matt. 16:14), but at the shadowed close of his own ministry
> it was to the sad, valiant story of Jeremiah's triumphant courage
> and deathless promise that the thoughts of Jesus turned. In the
> upper room, on the night on which he was betrayed, Jesus took
> the Passover cup and gave it to his disciples and quoted Jeremiah:
> "This cup is the *new covenant* sealed by my blood" (1 Cor. 11:25,
> NEB, emphasis mine). In that sublime moment all the darkness
> and rejection, the pain and self-doubt of Jeremiah's life were
> overlaid with radiance; all his service and suffering hallowed
> forever.
>
> A remarkable man indeed![35]

As we saw with Ezekiel, the Second Isaiah was deeply influenced by Jeremiah,
as were the Jewish people as a whole and, indeed, as were all the monotheistic
religions that came into being after the time of Jeremiah.

7.

Prophetic and Post-Prophetic Judaism

The literary prophets and Jeremiah in particular strove to have their people reach a stage of pure monotheism. One could argue that their expectations were unrealistic. Given the complexities and vicissitudes of life, one cannot maintain a high level of faith and ethical behavior at every moment. The human heart harbors doubts, fears, uncertainties, and is easy prey to temptation. Telling the truth at all times can present enormous problems, hence the term "white lie." To many, life seems overwhelming, hence the need to lean on someone or something. Above all, the fear of death causes people to look for answers beyond the here and now. When the Northern Kingdom of Israel was destroyed, its people were exiled and for the most part disappeared among the host nations. When Jerusalem fell to the Babylonians, the Judean exiles in Babylon and later in Persia and still later in the Hellenistic world began to adapt to the new reality of their life outside their land and a whole new process was set in motion of finding new answers to the old questions of human existence. Jeremiah stands between these two worlds—the old biblical world and the new post-exilic reality during which time the process of change of the faith and life of Israel is greatly accelerated.

As we saw in the previous chapter, radical changes were introduced almost as soon as the Babylonian Diaspora began, as reflected in the teachings of the prophet Ezekiel. Many more will soon follow, and some will endure to this day. Let us take a look at some of the key concepts that take hold of Judaism during the post-exilic period and assess them in the light of Jeremiah's teachings and the teachings of prophetic Judaism.

8.

Understanding God

The God of Jeremiah is absolute yet personal. There is no room in Jeremiah's universe for any other power besides God, whose name is not known to us yet is referred to as Adonai, or the Master of the Universe. Jeremiah never mentions angels, and he never mentions Satan. Angels are mentioned throughout the Bible, but we never have a clear idea as to their identity, their hierarchy, or their particular powers. The word angel in Hebrew is *mal'ach*, which means messenger. It performs God's will and acts as messenger of God who brings God's word to humans, beginning as early as the story of Adam and Eve. Angels in the biblical narrative are nebulous creatures who occupy a borderline between figments of one's imagination and an article of a belief system. Angels or divine beings appear in Isaiah's vision of God's presence (6:1-7), and in Ezekiel's vision of the heavenly chariot (1:5-27). In both visions God appears to the prophet and consecrates him for his mission. With Jeremiah it is altogether different. God appears to him in the simplest and most immediate way possible, as a voice heard when Jeremiah contemplates the blossoming almond tree. The danger with the belief in angels is that it lends itself to imputing to those beings divine powers in their own right, hence creating polytheism, or multiple gods. A case in point is a story regarding the "sons of God." It appears in the Bible's stories of creation, where mysterious creatures of this name fall in love with the daughters of man and marry them (Genesis 6:2). Who exactly are those "sons of God" is anyone's guess. By completely avoiding any mention of angels, Jeremiah seems to be aware of the danger of confusing angels as a metaphor with actual divine beings, hence infringing on the omnipotence of God.

The human desire to believe in angels, however, did not subside during or after the time of Jeremiah. On the contrary, it grew stronger. We find proof of it in Ezekiel's highly complex mystical vision of the chariot, which, along with the story of creation, forms the basis of Jewish mysticism, especially the Kabbalah. We find even more proof of it in the book of Daniel, in which for the first time angels are given names, such as Gabriel, who becomes an archangel, thus giving rise to a hierarchy of angels. Later, in Christianity, a whole science of angels will develop, known as angelology. Islam will also embrace angels, who will play a key role in Islamic theology. In Jewish lore, the angel of death plays a very prominent role, and is mentioned in the Passover Haggadah in the closing song of *Had gadya* (One Little Lamb). Rabbinical literature is full of stories of angels, most famously the two angels who accompany the Jew on the eve of the Sabbath, the good angel and the bad angel, each watching his behavior. Indeed, the idea of good and bad angels becomes well entrenched in world culture and religions both monotheistic and other, establishing a duality which flies in the face of monotheism.

This duality can be traced back to Persia, where some of the Judean exiles of the time of Jeremiah settle (see the book of Esther). Here we have Jews come under the influence of the Zoroaster religion, established in the sixth century BCE, which views the world as divided between two powers—good and evil, with two corresponding deities. Here we can find the beginnings of the rise of the most pernicious angel of all, namely, Satan, or the devil, who will become a key figure in both Christianity and Islam, as well as in post-biblical Judaism. A post-exilic biblical book, the book of Job, has Satan as a main character. Medieval Jewish commentators, such as Ibn Ezra, interpret the story of Adam and Eve and the "apple" (actually, "the fruit of the tree of the knowledge of good and evil") in such a way that the serpent becomes Satan, or the devil. No doubt, the idea of evil being represented in the world by a force other than the benevolent and loving God is one of the most powerful ideas that has ever taken hold of the human imagination. It does, however, create a duality that contradicts the idea of pure monotheism. In the story of Job, God has the final say over the actions of Satan, but the mere fact that Satan can persuade God to let him put Job, a perfectly righteous man, to the most severe tests, indicates that there is a power in the universe besides God that can cause some very serious harm.

In Jewish mysticism, Satan, known as the *sitra achrah*, or the other side, is a prominent player. But mainstream Judaism, beginning with post-biblical rabbinical Judaism, puts little stock on Satan, and prefers a different theory, namely, the *yetzer ha'ra*, or the evil inclination, which exists in every human being alongside the *yetzer ha'tov*, or the good inclination. Here responsibility is placed directly on the person, rather than an external force like Satan over whom one has no control. Without a doubt, given Jeremiah's character and his relationship with God, he would have much preferred the latter theory to the belief in a highly active Satan.

Jeremiah's understanding of God puts him centuries ahead of his time. It actually makes him a humanist and a rationalist (notwithstanding the fact that he is a highly emotional and sensitive person who is unconditionally loyal to God). Unlike Isaiah and Ezekiel, he does not engage in supernatural visions. Unlike an Elijah or an Elisha, he does not perform miracles. Unlike Daniel (whom Christians consider a prophet but Jews do not), he is not concerned with angels. While he is a visionary who predicts the return from Babylon and fully understands the historical dynamics of Jewish and world history, he is completely rooted in his place and time and does not spare any effort to save his people from their impending doom. To Jeremiah, his God-given mission in life is to help others, to put all selfish interest aside and champion human welfare while condemning human evil. To him, the Ten Commandments are not a goal to aspire to but rather a blueprint for living one must live by or else forfeit one's God-given rights. Jeremiah finds God in nature and in human affairs, past, present and future. His understanding of God as both a personal and a universal God is his greatest contribution to his people and to all people.

9.

Temple and Post-Temple Ritual

The idea of offering a sacrifice is deeply ingrained in the human condition. The word is derived from the Latin word *sacrificium*, to make holy. By giving of oneself or of one's possessions one becomes holy, or attains a spiritual level of grace. This belief was extended in all cultures and in all religions around the world to the relationship between the human and the divine, whereby God or—in the case of polytheistic religions—the gods, demands sacrifices. In the biblical story of the sacrifice of Isaac, God is testing Abraham by asking him to sacrifice his son on an altar on Mount Moriah. In other words, God is asking the first monotheist to offer a human sacrifice. This has been taken to mean that God was putting Abraham through a test of faith. Did Abraham pass the test? The official belief is that he did, for he was willing to give up that which was most precious to him because it was God's will. One, however, could argue that the real proof of faith would have been for Abraham to disagree with God and refuse to engage in the pagan practice of human sacrifice.[36] Be this as it may, the story goes on to say that at the last moment God prevented Abraham from sacrificing Isaac, and instead caused a ram to get caught in a thicket nearby. Abraham sacrifices the ram instead of his son, and thus Judaism embarks upon animal sacrifices as a substitute for human sacrifice.

Animal sacrifices remain the key ritual of the Hebrew faith until the destruction of the Second Temple. The bringing of offerings of both farm produce and livestock to the places of worship, particularly to the *bet ha'mikdash* or the Holy Temple in Jerusalem, becomes the main source of livelihood for the priestly class, which is far from small. The priests, one would assume, were very pleased with this system. Not so the prophets. From the prophetic standpoint, there seems to be an ongoing conflict between ritual and moral conduct. Not a single prophet during some five centuries from the time of Samuel to the time of Jeremiah appears to be pleased with the moral conduct of either the king or the people. During that entire period the sacrificial cult is alive and well, but the prophets are routinely inveighing against immorality and its twin sister, idolatry. Obviously, the common belief among the Hebrews is that as long as one brings offerings to the priests, everything else is forgiven. Not so, says the prophet. "It has been told you, O man, what is good," the prophet Micah reminds his people, "and what Adonai your God expects of you, but to do justly, and to love mercy, and to walk humbly with Adonai your God" (6:8).

Jeremiah is no different in this respect. On the contrary, his entire prophetic career is dedicated to excoriating his people for their immorality and idolatry.

From the beginning of his career he decries the smugness of his people who bring offerings to the Temple in Jerusalem while practicing idolatry in the privacy of their homes and immorality both in private and in public. And yet, neither Jeremiah nor any of the other prophets ever calls for the abolition of the sacrificial cult. They all accept it as part of the Mosaic Law, particularly as enunciated in the book of Leviticus. When Jeremiah sees the end of the Kingdom of Judah drawing near, he begins to offer prophecies of consolation and hope in which a main component is the restoration of the priests and the Levites and the temple cult. So does his successor, Ezekiel, who goes a step further and offers a detailed description of the rebuilding of the Holy Temple in Jerusalem. And yet, after the fall of Jerusalem and the burning of the Temple, there is no longer a place to offer sacrifices. A very touching story in the book of Jeremiah is the one about the group of people who come down from Samaria with offerings to the Temple, presumably because they haven't yet found out that the Temple is no longer standing.

For about a hundred years, between the time of the beginning of the Babylonian exile and the return of the exiles to Jerusalem under Ezra and Nehemiah when the Temple is rebuilt and the sacrifices are resumed, something new and of critical significance for the future takes place. Prayer, the study of Torah, and the intensified observance of such commandments as the dietary laws and the Sabbath take hold of the exiles in Babylon, who bring them back with them to Jerusalem. Much evidence of all of this is found in the books of Ezra and Nehemiah. Ezra introduces the reading of the Law in public. Nehemiah is a pious Jew who regularly prays to God. Another Judean in Babylon, namely, Daniel, is very careful about keeping the dietary laws, and so on. While the Temple and its sacrificial cult are restored, Judaism is no longer the same. When the Second Temple is destroyed by the Romans nearly six hundred years later, the leading rabbi of the time, Rabbi Johanan ben Zakkai, does not look upon the destruction of the Temple as a national calamity—though to this day it has been viewed by Jews as the greatest national tragedy of Jewish history—but rather as a historical necessity. By then, the synagogue and the house of study have already replaced the Temple, and Judaism continues to live on and reaches a higher spiritual level without the Temple and the sacrificial cult, but rather as a religion that emphasizes the study of Torah, prayer, and *gemilut hasadim*, or charitable and good deeds. To Johanan ben Zakkai and his colleagues, the founders of rabbinical Judaism, it was clear that the Temple and the animal sacrifices were standing in the way of the new, much more advanced and much more sophisticated Judaism. How to explain the paradox of a people moving into a new stage of their spiritual development yet yearning for the old stage which is no longer viable? One answer is tradition. The British still have a monarchy, although in practical terms it has little meaning. They just refuse to give it up. Similarly, ultra-Orthodox Jews still study all the laws of the sacrifices in the Torah and pray every day for the restoration of the Temple. Jeremiah may agree with them, or he may not. We may never know.

Medieval Jewish philosophers differ in their view on the issue of the sacrifices. Thus, the highly rational Moses Maimonides does not believe that there is much point in the sacrifices being reinstated. He considers them inferior to prayer, a concession God originally made to the Hebrews in turning them from paganism to monotheism. Other medieval Jewish philosophers, such as Nachmanides and Judah Halevi, disagree. They see the sacrifices central to Judaism, a ritual practice that will be restored when the messiah comes and the Temple is rebuilt. Most Jews today tend to side with Maimonides rather than with those who express the opposite view.

10.

Messianism

It is common among the Hebrew prophets to envision a time when their people truly return to God and attain redemption. In this regard, Jeremiah is no exception. But the idea takes on different forms and different degrees of intensity. In post-biblical Jewish history, this idea takes on great urgency at certain times, particularly during periods of great national crisis or cataclysmic events. In time, this idea will evolve into a Jewish belief in a future messiah who will come and redeem his people through supernatural means. The idea of a messiah has its origins in a perfectly natural event related to the monarchic period, namely, the anointing of a king. The word messiah is derived from the Hebrew verb m-sh-h, namely, to anoint. The kings, beginning with Saul and David, were anointed with consecrated oil as part of the ceremony of transmitting to the person God-given authority.

The prophets lived during the monarchic period which, according to the biblical account, was characterized for the most part by kings and their subjects failing to live up to the standards of the covenant. As a result, the prophets found themselves comparing their contemporary monarch with King David, the one beloved by God.[37] David remains the model king in prophetic literature. God's promise that the House of David will remain on the throne forever was accepted by the prophets as one of history's enduring truths, and the prophets eventually began to talk about the "shoot from the root of David" (Isaiah 11:1) who will rule at a future time when the covenant will be fully implemented. Jeremiah is no exception to this rule. One of his favorite terms is "the throne of David" (17:25, 22:2, 29:16, 36:30), implying that the only reason the kings of his time (with the exception of Josiah) sat on that throne was because of David, their common progenitor. Jeremiah makes the following unequivocal statement:

> Thus says Adonai: If My covenant with the day
> and with the night be annulled so that there will
> be neither day nor night in its appointed time,
> then will my covenant with My servant David be
> annulled so that he will not have a son ruling on
> his throne.   (33:20-21)

In other words, the laws of nature will have to change before God changes His promise to David.

When the exiles return from Babylonian exile in the time of Ezra and Nehemiah, they are not able to reestablish the Davidic monarchy. Their patron, King Cyrus of Persia, does not authorize them to establish a monarchy, only a theocracy. The belief in the reinstatement of the Davidic dynasty, however, does not disappear. It is only deferred. In time, it will become sublimated, and by the time of the destruction of the Second Temple it is no longer a political but rather an eschatological belief in a future messiah who will come to redeem his people and the world, resurrect the dead, and bring about the messianic era. It is around the same time that Christianity separates from Judaism and becomes a religion based on the belief that the messiah has already come and has brought redemption to all those willing to believe in him.

Needless to say, the Christian belief in a redeemer whom God has sent into the world to bring individual salvation to all who are willing to accept him is a most powerful belief, for it has and continues to impact on the lives of millions of people around the world. But to take a leap of faith from Jeremiah's words to this belief is not entirely sustainable. In our foregoing discussion of Jeremiah's concept of God it was made clear that he had no room in his monotheistic faith for anyone else except the one God of the Universe. Neither the later concept of a Jewish messiah who will redeem the world through supernatural means, much less a Christian messiah who is believed to be a divine being fits in with Jeremiah's thinking. To him the descendant of the House of David remains a human ruler pure and simple who, some day, will ascend to the throne of David. Whether or not this will ever happen remains to be seen.

11.

Afterlife and Resurrection

Afterlife

The word paradise is derived from the Greek word *paradeisos*, which means an enclosed garden. From the dawn of time, humans have dreamed of paradise. The belief in a place—either this-worldly or other-worldly—where people have no cares, where all their needs are taken care of, and where one lives in an endless state of bliss, is reflected in the biblical story of the first human couple, who lives like innocent children in an enclosed garden called the Garden of Eden. What is remarkable about the Hebrew Bible in general and about the Hebrew prophets in particular is that no attempt is being made anywhere in the text to look for, specu-late about, or reestablish that place called paradise, either in this life or in an afterlife. Ancient Israel was not concerned with an afterlife, but rather with life here and now. The good life meant living a life of righteousness in peace and prosperity, having offspring, dying in peace, being buried with one's forebears, and leaving a good name. Similar to the ancient Greeks, the Hebrews did have folk beliefs about the afterlife, in which the soul of the dead existed in a nebulous netherworld called *she'ol* in Hebrew or Hades in Greek. When a distraught King Saul wishes to talk to the dead prophet Samuel, he goes to see the woman of En-Dor who conjures up Samuel's soul from the dead. The prophets, however, frown upon such beliefs. Their teachings make it clear time and again that life is here and now, and anything beyond this life is in the hands of God and not for man to be concerned with. We read in the book of Psalms:

> The dead do not praise God,
> Nor those who go down into silence. (115:17)

Jeremiah never mentions or intimates an afterlife. He is well within the He-brew prophetic tradition when it comes to this belief. Yet soon after his time the belief begins to take hold of his people,[38] and will eventually become a belief in what rabbinical Judaism calls *olam ha'bah*, the world to come. The Talmud, com-posed during the first five centuries of the common era, makes numerous refer-ences to the next life. The most striking of these statements is the one that refers to this life as the corridor that leads to the main room, which is the next life.[39] In this next life there are two domains—*gan eden*, or paradise, and *gehinom*, or hell. The name for paradise is derived, to be sure, from the genesis stories, while the name for hell is derived from a physical place outside Jerusalem, the Valley of

Hinom, which was considered an evil place in biblical times, and particularly in the time of Jeremiah, because it was the site of pagan rituals such as passing children through fire prior to Josiah's Reform, although the nature of this place remains obscure.

In Christianity, paradise and hell, or heaven and hell, become key beliefs from the very beginning. In fact, beginning with the concept of the "kingdom of heaven" in the Gospels, where the poor and the humble are promised that "theirs is the kingdom of heaven" (Sermon on the Mount), Christianity's main promise to its followers is that no matter how unhappy their lot in this world may be, there is a next world or a next life where the righteous will live a life of eternal bliss. The wicked, on the other hand, will find themselves in a place of eternal suffering and damnation. This is, indeed, a very powerful belief. It solves two key problems of human existence—the injustice of this life, and its brevity. There are, however, two problems with this belief: first, there is absolutely no proof of the existence of an eternal life and either a heaven or a hell, and second, by shifting the meaning of human existence from this life to another, unknown life, one can accept evil, injustice and all the ills of this life as a given, and rather than work to eliminate them, one can assume an attitude of doing nothing and waiting for that other life to start.

In Judaism, as we see in various statements of the post-biblical period, the belief in an afterlife never becomes a central or critical component of the Jewish belief system. It is relegated to the realm of the *aggadah*, or moral fable. In one place the Talmud raises the question as to what the righteous do in heaven. The answer is, they attend a heavenly Torah academy, where they sit in a circle with a halo over their head and learn Torah directly from the Divine Presence.[40]

The implication here is quite clear: the learning of Torah is the highest value, and it contains within it eternal life. This is true in this life, and may be true in the next if indeed there is an afterlife. Nevertheless, the emphasis in Judaism remains to this day on life here and now. The religious laws the Jew lives by focus on life from birth to death or, in more technical terms, from circumcision to the burial rite. The world, the Talmud states, stands on three pillars: the study of Torah, prayer, and good deeds. All three have to do with life here and now, none has to do with a next life. Here Jeremiah would feel perfectly at home, whereas shifting the emphasis of human life from this life to an afterlife is something with which Jeremiah would feel quite uncomfortable.

Resurrrection of the Dead

The other seemingly critical belief of post-exilic (or rather post-biblical) Judaism is the resurrection of the dead. In Judaism this belief is tied to the time of the coming of the messiah. In the book of Ezekiel we find the famous vision of the resurrection of the dry bones (37:1-14). Ezekiel, Jeremiah's successor, finds himself in a valley full of dry bones. God asks him: Can these dry bones come back to life? Ezekiel is overwhelmed by the question and replies that only God knows the answer. God orders Ezekiel to summon the wind from the four corners of the earth and blow the breath of life into the dry bones. While this vision has been taken by later generations—particularly by Christian scholars—to confirm the resurrection of the dead, Ezekiel makes it clear that the story is a fable designed to dramatize Jeremiah's prophecies about the return of the Babylonian exiles to their land, referred to by Ezekiel as "the soil of Israel" (37:12).

Jewish scholars and philosophers such as Maimonides have had difficulties with the belief in physical resurrection. Even though Maimonides includes this belief in his list of the thirteen basic beliefs of Judaism, he kept avoiding discussing it in detail in his writings about the principles of the Jewish faith, which led to many attacks against him led by key Jewish scholars of his time and forcing him late in life to write a treatise about the subject.[41] One does not need to be an ecologist to know that if every person that has ever lived came back to life it would be impossible for planet earth to sustain such a population of countless billions. In another mode of non-physical existence or in another dimension of being one could perhaps make a case for such resurrection, but certainly not in the simple natural reality of life as we know it.

In summarizing such beliefs as messianism, afterlife and resurrection, it is clear that they all result from the innermost yearnings and concerns of the human heart. As to their validity, that is a matter of faith rather than fact. People choose to believe in many things. As long as these things help them cope with their lives without hurting others, all is good and well. When such beliefs become the cause of prejudice and violence, as we see happening all too often even in the twenty-first century, they accomplish the exact opposite of what they were meant to accomplish. This is the inherent danger of beliefs that are not anchored in actual human experience but rather in the yearnings of the human heart.

12.

Chosen People

Practically every national or religious group on the planet at one time or another or in one form or another has come to regard itself as God's chosen people. No doubt the Assyrians and the Babylonians and the Egyptians and the Romans did, and in our time the Germans and the Japanese and many others also have, with disastrous consequences. And the same applies to religious groups old and new. Very wealthy people tend to see themselves as chosen, and so do very poor people, who need a good reason to cope with their lot. Seeing oneself as chosen is part of the human condition. When it comes to the Jews, however, it is another matter. For centuries, the Jews have been accused, mainly by the Church, of setting themselves up as God's chosen people, hence acting superior to others. The fact remains that since the day the Church established itself as the supreme authority of Western civilization some sixteen centuries ago, it was the Church that acted as God's chosen, while the Jews for the most part were treated as inferior people and were subjected to many forms of persecution. All of this, of course, came to its most horrific climax in the death camps of Europe during the Second World War. The term "chosen people" as applied to the Jews is one of the most insidious and disastrous terms ever invented.

What does Jeremiah have to say about the idea of a chosen people? One would be very hard put to find evidence of Jeremiah thinking of his people as the so-called chosen people. If the word chosen means better or superior, Jeremiah, who loves his people passionately (although for the most part they didn't love him back, at least not during his lifetime), never once refers to them as chosen or superior. On the contrary, he constantly compares them unfavorably to other nations who display virtues his own people lack. Other nations remain loyal to their own gods while the people of Israel and Judah keep betraying their God (2:10-11). It may be true that Jeremiah and the other prophets hold their own people up to higher moral standards than they do other people, but this is because the Hebrews were introduced to a moral and religious code that made certain demands on them which they failed to live up to time and again. When God makes the covenant with Israel, God expects them to become "A kingdom of priests and a holy nation" (Exodus 19:6). Instead, they choose to have a king over them, and fail to live up to the standards that constitute holiness.

The covenant, however, between God and Israel remains in effect not because the people are worthy of it, but because—according to the prophets, God wills it. One could speculate that if another people were more worthy of the covenant, God may have given up on Israel and chosen another people. But apparently that has not been the case.[42] The historical record shows that every national, ethnic or religious group on this earth has engaged in bloodshed, immorality and idolatry. There has been little reason since homo erectus began to walk this earth and homo sapiens began to form human communities to have any particular group singled out as the one to be given the knowledge of monotheism. Hence one could speculate that either God chose the Hebrews arbitrarily, or because their forebear, Abraham, was the first human worthy of it, or that it was not God who chose the Hebrews, but rather the Hebrews who chose God. Once that happened, it became their destiny to be God's witnesses among the nations, and that destiny, as Jeremiah reminds us throughout his long prophetic career, has, for better or for worse, stuck with them, and continues to be their destiny to this day.

13.

Self and Community

The process of religious and ethical individuation in Judaism begins with Jeremiah. Until his time, the Hebrews are a tribal people. The identity of the individual is subsumed under the identity of one's family within one's tribe. When a member of the tribe of Benjamin rapes the concubine of a member of the tribe of Levi during the time of the Judges, all the other tribes declare war on the tribe of Benjamin, kill thousands of Benjaminites, and nearly put that tribe out of existence (Judges 19-21). Guilt, in other words, is collective rather than individual. The biblical writer of this story makes the comment that in those days there was no king in Israel, and people took the law into their own hands. But even during the monarchic period the Hebrew society remained tribal. Only two kings—David and Solomon—managed to keep the tribes together, but after the death of Solomon the kingdom split in two and continued to live along tribal lines.

When the prophets address their people, they invariably address them as a society, or a community, not as individuals. Amos talks about the fat cows of Bashan when he addresses the rich women of Samaria who have no regard for the poor (4:1). Isaiah addresses the people of Jerusalem who will hopefully one day return to God (1:26). Jeremiah does the same when he talks to the people of Judah and excoriates them for their idolatry and immorality. Yet Jeremiah is the first prophet who begins to talk about individual responsibility when he says:

> In those days they shall no longer say: The fathers have
> eaten sour grapes and the children's teeth are blunted.
> Everyone shall die for his own sins; every person that
> eats the sour grapes his teeth shall be blunted.
> (31:29-30)

Jeremiah understands that once Jerusalem is destroyed and the people are exiled, they will no longer be able to survive under the tribal system. The tribal existence is predicated on a territory occupied by the tribe. Once exiled, the people have to survive as individuals and as a faith, rather than as tribes or even a nation. The three elements of Jewish individual and communal existence are: the study of the Torah, prayer, and the performance of charitable deeds. All of this can be done without a cultic center such as a temple, and without the cult of animal sacrifices. Jeremiah refers to the study of the Torah when he criticizes the priests and the teachers of the Torah (the ones who "hold the Torah" [2:8]) for failing to make the Torah part of the life of the people. We also find him praying to God in order to receive answers to his questions. Others before him, like Solomon or Hannah, the mother of Samuel, also prayed to God. But with Jeremiah prayer begins to take on a new meaning because of his intimate relationship with God. Finally, like all the other prophets, Jeremiah also talks about moral and charitable behavior, which is at the heart and core of the religion of the Hebrew society, even in its tribal form.

Ezekiel, Jeremiah's prophetic successor, takes the process of individuation a step further by arguing

> All souls are Mine; the soul of the father
> and the soul of the son are Mine;
> the soul that sins, it shall die. (18:1-4)

In other words, individual responsibility, which Jeremiah placed in the future, is now taking place in the present among the Judean exiles in Babylon. From now on, each one of them is responsible for his or her own destiny in a direct relationship between the individual person and God.

When the young David is forced to flee from his country because of the jealousy of King Saul who seeks to kill him, he asks God how he will be able to receive God's favor and protection while away from his own country. In other words, to David, God is territorial. Once in Philistia, David does not feel he is under the protection of the God of Israel:

> They have driven me out this day that
> I may not have a share in Adonai's possession,
> saying, Go serve other gods. (I Samuel 26:19)

This kind of thinking changes completely at the time of the exile, immediately after the time of Jeremiah. When the young Daniel of the royal house in Jerusalem is exiled to Babylon, he finds ways to observe his religion despite the threats made against him. When the Judean Mordecai who lives in Persian exile has to assert his Jewish faith, he manages to do so in the face of the grave threat made by Haman, the Persian king's counselor, who seeks to destroy him and all the rest of the Jews in the Persian Empire.

It is remarkable how quickly, following the destruction of the Kingdom of Judah, the Judean exiles were able to acquire a new communal and individual identity based on a non-territorial communal existence, in which the community is essential for the study of the Torah, for prayer, and for moral and charitable conduct, and at the same time it enables the individual Jew to operate and survive as an individual. This new reality is at the core of the survival of the Jew as a member of a rather small people in the midst of much larger societies and much more wide-spread cultures. Jewish life over time takes root in remote countries and communities, such as Yemen, Ethiopia, India, and later in the New World in remote places like Curaçao, Barbados and Jamaica. And despite numeric inferiority, hostility, and persecution by the dominant culture or religion, and the seductive influence of the culturally and physically more powerful host cultures, this small people has not only been able to keep its identity, but has also been able to continue its development and its creative existence, with great writers, artists, thinkers, scientists, and religious luminaries making contributions to their own culture and to world culture throughout the ages, and ultimately has had the staying power and the determination to do something no other people has ever done, namely, return to its ancestral land a second time in twenty-five centuries and once again begin a productive and creative life in the present-day state of Israel.

14.

Jeremiah's Universality

One of the strangest prophecies in the book of Jeremiah is the one known as the Vision of the Cup (25:15-38). This vision, in which God orders Jeremiah to take a wine cup and force all the nations of the world to drink from it, raises many questions as to its precise authorship, later redactions, and final editing. Unlike Jeremiah's other prophecies, it is written in prose rather than poetry. Its style is complex and confusing. It starts with a long list of the nations and cities God asks Jeremiah to go to and serve this cup of wine, called "the wine of anger" or "the wine of poison." The purpose of drinking this wine is to cause the leaders of those nations to become drunk and to be poisoned, so that they may lose control of themselves and their affairs of state, and their erratic behavior results in world chaos and conflict, leading to a worldwide war and destruction. The message here seems clear: the affairs of humankind are not controlled by kings and rulers, but by a higher force.

Clearly, this is not a realistic scenario, but rather a flight of the imagination. One tends to attach to it the label "eschatological," or a prophecy having to do with the end of the world or the end of humankind, which is quite atypical of Jeremiah but more typical of his successor, Ezekiel. The idea of a judgment day is common to the Hebrew prophets, who most of the time refer to it as "the day of Adonai," or, in past English translations, "the day of the Lord."[43] The day of Adonai is that unknown future time when judgment will be visited upon Israel as well as upon the nations. In time, this idea will evolve into both the Jewish and the Christian eschatology of the end of time and the messianic era. In other words, the time when Jews expect to have their messiah redeem them and perhaps also the rest of humankind, and Christians expect *their* messiah to come back a second time and redeem *them* and perhaps also the rest of the world. Interestingly, Jeremiah never mentions "the day of Adonai."

It is somewhat difficult to attribute to Jeremiah any kind of an eschatological leaning, since everything he has to say is so rooted in reality. When it comes to his prophecies to the nations, however, it is never fully clear what he is looking to accomplish. We do not have the same problem with his prophecies to his own people. Here his purpose is clear and straightforward: combat idolatry and immorality, and return to the covenant. When it comes to his various prophecies to the nations things always seem to become muddled. First, it is clear that most of the time he is not quite sure exactly which nation or nations he is addressing. At times, hespeaks in generalities. Other times he mentions nations he may have heard of but is not quite sure who they are, and neither are we. This vagueness is best seen early on in his prophecies about "the enemy from the north," which we have discussed at length earlier in the book. One must go back to God's original call to Jeremiah, where the young boy is commanded to become a "prophet to the nations," in addition to being a prophet to his own people. Well, Jeremiah must have said to himself as he grew up, how exactly do I go about being a prophet to the nations? And so he starts with the "enemy from the north," continues with the Vision of the Cup, and finally compiles an anthology of prophecies to the nations, while in exile in Egypt before he dies, which once again do not shed much additional light on what exactly he is trying to accomplish.

The foregoing may sound as a caustic and irreverent assessment of Jeremiah's prophecies to the nations, which this author, as one of Jeremiah's greatest admirers, would rather not be accused of. But since I made a pledge at the outset to be completely honest in my treatment of this subject, I feel obliged to make this observation. But I do believe there is much more here than meets the eye. Jeremiah, like his predecessor Isaiah, and like other biblical prophets, grasped intuitively two things: one, the fate of the entire human race is bound together, and second, that idea finds its ultimate expression in a place called Jerusalem, where the true God of the Universe became known to the world, making it the focal point of the destiny of humankind. This is the motif that appears in all of Jeremiah's prophecies to the nations. The "enemy from the north," a coalition of kings, would come and lay siege to Jerusalem. This will happen more than a few times throughout history. The Vision of the Cup also begins in Jerusalem. The prophecies against Babylon have to do with God's punishment reserved for that nation that destroyed Jerusalem. And the prophecies to the nations are tied to the Vision of the Cup (49:12).

Jeremiah and the other biblical prophets did not have the kind of information or communication, or the kind of knowledge that would have enabled them to become experts on world affairs. Much of what they had to say about this subject was based on indirect and often inaccurate information, and on pure intuition. They could often err when it came to technical details. Theirs was not a scientific vision, but rather a moral one. It would be a mistake to try to study the geography or the international political scene of their time from their utterances. But they were entirely correct in grasping the common destiny of the human race, and in articulating their moral vision that was based on their monotheistic insights.

To limit Jeremiah's and the other prophets' teachings to the small nation of Israel, or to its descendants, as Jewish commentators, scholars, thinkers, and religious leaders have done throughout time, is wrong. They were prophets to the world, even as the God they envisioned, the God of universal justice, mercy and love is not a parochial or territorial deity, but the one and only God of the Universe, to whom all human beings, regardless of color or race, all created in the image of God, are equal and the same. It is equally wrong to relegate them to the ancillary role of mere harbingers whose historical mission was to prepare the way for a future prophet or messiah, who would bring the world the ultimate truth. They did not look to replace the faith of their own people with a new faith from another source or another part of the human race. To them the covenant between God and the Jewish people was immutable and irreplaceable. That other nations should find the knowledge of the one God through their own teachers or through someone they believe to be their prophet, is something that goes beyond the purview of what they set out to accomplish. It is very instructive, indeed, that after centuries during which the doctrine of the Church maintained that the covenant between God and Israel was replaced by a new covenant, finally, in our time, the Vatican has amended its doctrine by stating that the old covenant between God and Israel continues to remain in effect alongside the new Christian covenant. This is an enormous step forward in the healing process between the mother and the daughter religions.[44]

Both Isaiah and Jeremiah, as well as Micah, in their respective visions of the end of days when the nations of the world will come to Jerusalem and will ask to be instructed in the ways of the God of Israel, make it clear that the vision of a world at peace is not a vision of a world which is religiously monolithic, but rather pluralistic. The nations of the world will not all join one religion. Rather, each will have its own understanding the reality of one world under one God, even as within all the major religions there are many differing beliefs, observances, and interpretations. The idea of the many paths to God was completely clear to the prophets, as it was to the rabbis who succeeded them. It is clear to every reasonable person in every culture and religion. It is only the extremists, who unfortunately can be found everywhere, who deny others the right to think differently and practice their faith in a different way. Tolerance and the acceptance of the rights of others are at the heart of the prophetic teachings.

Chapter Three

What Would Jeremiah Have to Say to Us Today?

1.

Choose Life, Choose Peace

If we were to ask Jeremiah what message he has for us today, he would open the book of Deuteronomy to chapter 30, verse 19, and he would read us the following words:

> Today, as heaven and earth are my witnesses,
> I have put before you life and death,
> Blessing and curse.
> Therefore choose life
> That you and your seed my live.

Choose life—these words are spoken by Moses as he prepares his people for the crossing of the Jordan River into the Promised Land. As we have seen throughout the book of Jeremiah, God always gives people a choice between right and wrong. All of life is choosing. This was true thirty-three centuries ago in the time of Moses, twenty-six centuries ago in the time of Jeremiah, and it is true today. If Jeremiah came back today and were introduced to the history of the past one hundred years, he would have to conclude that the human race during this past century has made many more wrong than right choices. Over time, these wrong choices, which have included many violent conflicts, have created permanent anger, hatred, resentment, and grievances between peoples and nations. The twentieth century started with a great promise of a world at peace, bringing prosperity to large numbers of people. But it turned out to be the bloodiest of all the centuries the human race has ever known. During the twentieth century, many new ideologies sought to replace the ideologies of the past with what may be defined as secular versions of traditional messianism, implemented by human leaders who

149

sought to transform the destiny of their people. Hundreds of millions of people died in the name of national redemption, social justice, brotherhood, and equality. They died in the name of national-socialism, capitalism, fascism, communism and so on. They died without bringing about a better world. Not only has the twentieth century failed to bring about a better world, it brought misery and death to countless millions on every continent. To Jews, it brought the greatest catastrophe in their entire history, namely, the Holocaust.

On the other hand, the twentieth century also saw many nations become independent for the first time, and millions who lived under foreign rule or the rule of the minority took their destiny into their own hands and became independent. Furthermore, the twentieth century saw the first man on the moon, unprecedented medical progress, and a digital age that has only begun to transform the future.

Still, we have now started a new century full of violent conflicts, and we are living in a world suffering from extreme inequality and poverty, huge ecological problems, old ethnic animosities we fail to resolve, and a host of other problems.

We do not have a Jeremiah in our midst. It is no longer fashionable for leaders, religious or secular, to insist that they receive divine messages. Those who do are held up to ridicule by level-headed people, and rightly so. But we do have the teachings of Jeremiah and the Hebrew prophets, and those teachings are timeless. None of the ideologies of the past one hundred years has replaced them. They continue to speak to us today as they spoke to people since the day the words "choose life" were first spoken. All we have to do is to listen and learn. As we bring this book to a close, let us ask ourselves what would Jeremiah have to say about the critical issues we face in the new century?

Life

Human life is the most sacred value of all. In the twentieth century, secular ideologies sacrificed the lives of hundreds of millions of people in the name of an ostensible higher value, such as nationalism or a utopian socialist state. The cynical explanation that became prevalent during that time was "the end justifies the means." For years, people accepted this assertion, and it took two world wars for the world to learn that the end never justifies the means. Any system that makes human life a secondary value is doomed to fail. The individual does not exist for the sake of the state. The state exists for the sake of the individual. When an American president declared in his inaugural speech, "Ask not what your country can do for you; ask what you can do for your country," he did not mean to say that country comes before the individual person, but rather that it is in the best interest of every individual to contribute to the common good, so that the strong can help the weak and all may benefit. He did not say, "U.S. *über alles*, the U.S. above all else." He sought to build a new frontier of social justice and a U.S. that helps other countries through such ventures as a Peace Corps, an Alliance for Progress, and so on. An assassin's bullet cut his vision short.

Nearly half a century after John F. Kennedy was assassinated, his vision is still far from being fulfilled. Regard for human life continues to be at an all-time low in many parts of the world, and the plague of international terrorism has cast a pall across the entire planet. Human rights are being violated everywhere, including in countries that are fighting international terrorism and seek to promote freedom and democracy.

No cause in the world justified the inhumane treatment of prisoners, much less the cold-blooded starving or murder of an innocent child. Yet innocent children are being starved and killed every day. Every innocent child who dies anywhere on the planet constitutes a crime against life itself, a grim reminder that not all that much progress has been made since the time of Cain and Abel.

The world Jeremiah knew had blood on its hands. No society in his day was exempt, not even his own. Today's world is no different. We all have blood on our hands. Not only those who do the killing, but also the rest of us, who routinely stand by and do nothing about it. When Adam cheats God and eats the forbidden fruit, God says to Adam, "Where are you?" God knows exactly where Adam is. But what God is really asking is, "Where are you as a moral human being?" God continues to ask us this question to this day, and we do not have a good answer.

Jeremiah excoriates all the nations of his time. All are guilty, most of all his own people. Unlike some religious leaders of the various major religions in our time, he does not extol his own people and faith and damns the others. His God does not take sides. For his God is the God of universal justice. His God sits in judgment of every living being, and we need to sit in judgment of ourselves.

Once we all agree that life is the highest value, everything else will begin to fall into place.

Peace

All people on this planet yearn for peace, yet everywhere one looks there are violent conflicts flaring up like brushfire, and at least one such conflict at any given moment turns into a full scale war. In the time of the prophets the beginning of spring was called in Hebrew "the time of the going out of the kings" (I Chronicles 20:1). What it meant was that, routinely, when the weather began to clear up, kings gathered their armies and went to war. This has been true not only of the ancient Near East, but also of every place and time from the tropical islands of the

South Pacific to the frozen steppes of Mongolia. One must wonder whether tribes and nations are capable of living in peace for any extended periods of time, or whether humanity is doomed to exist in a perpetual state of war.

The root causes of war are well known. There are territorial wars, in which a disputed territory is fought over. There are religious or ideological wars, in which one religion or ideology looks to impose itself on another. There are economical wars, in which a physical resource such as food, water, or a mineral is the *casus belli*. Moreover, poverty and hunger are fertile ground for human conflict.

The territorial cause may be the most problematic cause of all. Many wars are fought because people run out of living space or *Lebensraum*, and need to reclaim land through aggressive means. This happens when a population in a particular area exceeds the ability of that area to sustain life. This happens in the animal kingdom on a regular basis. In today's world, affluent countries suffer from a low birth rate, while poor countries suffer from a very high birth rate. The world's population in the past fifty years has grown threefold, from two to over six billion. This does not bode well for the future.

It would follow, then, that in a world where all these various kinds of conflicts are resolved, peace will become possible. This, of course, is easier said than done. So far, the first decade of the twenty-first century has been punctuated by a wide-range of violent conflicts—ethnic-cleansing in the Balkans; genocides in parts of Africa like Rwanda and Darfur; domestic terrorism from the Russian province of Chechnia to Spain; and an international outburst of Islamic terrorism that gave the United States its first major foreign terrorist attack on its own soil. Last but not least, the conflicts in the Middle East, most of them internecine, continue. The specter of atomic weapons in the hands of politically or religiously fanatic regimes such as the ones in Iran and in North Korea has begun to cast a long shadow around the world.

There is, however, another side to the coin. The nations of Europe, with the help of the United States, stopped the ethnic cleansing in the Balkans and managed to bring a terrible situation under control; Darfur has become a center of world attention, and the Sudanese government has not been able to continue to act there with impunity; the Arab world is no longer monolithic in its support of Islamic extreme causes and regimes; and forces of moderation in many of its countries are actively searching for solutions. Europe, the main venue of the two world wars, is unifying. All these are encouraging signs of a shift of thinking around the world. Rational people everywhere are aware of the common dangers our planet faces, and in the long run rational people, rather than hotheads, prevail.

On the other hand, there are many people who have despaired of ever seeing a world at peace, and with good reason. Many have lost faith in the human ability to live in peace. People look around themselves and see much more selfishness than willingness to work for the common good. They see people everywhere with little or no regard for human life, particularly for the lives of those they perceive to be their enemies. They feel helpless about effecting any change. And so they give up.

Jeremiah was not a prophet of despair. He may have acquired a reputation over the centuries as a prophet of gloom and doom, but this is a misconception. He lived in the midst of a doomed society, a society unaware of its own impending doom. But he never despaired of the possibility of bringing his people around, even after the destruction of Jerusalem. He believed in the future of his people, and he believed in the future of the human race. Like Isaiah and Micah before him, he envisioned a time when his own people and the nations of the world would come together in Jerusalem and

> At that time they will call Jerusalem the seat of Adonai,
> And all the nations will gather there for the sake of
> Adonai in Jerusalem. And they will no longer follow
> the stubbornness of their evil heart. (3:17)

Jeremiah is not talking about any cataclysmic events preceding such a time. He sees great wars and destruction as he prophesies to the nations, but he is not eschatological and certainly not supernatural about it. What he actually appears to be saying is that human beings have the capacity to bring about an age of reconciliation and peaceful coexistence. He does not need a mythical messiah to do it for them. God has given the human race a great gift, namely, the human brain, and God expects people to use it. The whole human race today is connected through digital technology as if it were one small village, whereby hamlets deep inside the Amazon have satellite dishes and can watch world news, remote islands around the globe can e-mail to anyone around the world, and cell phones connect people around the globe. The world has become completely transparent, and people everywhere have the ability to do something about the tsunami in Indonesia (and they have), or about the massacres in Darfur (and they do), or about anything else in the world. There is new hope in the midst of today's seemingly insoluble problems.

In my lifetime, the Jewish people went through the worst tragedy in their history, followed by the greatest redemption. Once again they are living proof to the presence of God in history. The tragedy led to redemption. Despite all those who try to deny the tragedy as well as the redemption, the world has taken notice of it, and it has prompted the United Nations to take a stand against genocides everywhere. As for the redemption, there are those who do not believe it will last.

Jeremiah would say to those people: It can last, but the people of Israel have to earn it. God is still watching, like that day when that young boy first heard the voice of God out of the almond tree. And God expects certainly things from the people of the covenant. Even the freethinking founder of the State of Israel, David Ben-Gurion, believed this to be true.

World peace will not happen overnight. There are too many things that are wrong with our world. But conflicts can be brought under control, and, to paraphrase Jeremiah, destruction will be followed by rebuilding and replanting, One has to believe that the will exists among people everywhere to move the world away from war and toward peace, and that the forces of light will triumph over the forces of darkness.

2.

Was Jeremiah a Pacifist?

In 1917, at the height of World War One, the Austrian Jewish writer Stefan Zweig wrote a stirring anti-war play called *Jeremiah*, in which he portrayed the prophet as a pacifist. Premiered in Switzerland, the play was performed in New York in 1939, on the eve of World War Two. By that time, Zweig had fled Austria because of the Nazi takeover, and found refuge in Brazil, where he committed suicide.

Zweig was a pacifist. Jeremiah was not. Pacifism appears in the Hebrew Bible only as a vision of a future time, best enunciated by Isaiah in his prophecies of the end of days. Isaiah's most famous statement is the following:

> Nation shall not lift up sword against nation,
> Neither shall they learn war any more. (2:4)

With the birth of utopian movements in the past two centuries, either secular or religious, the idea of active or practical pacifism came into the world, and has been pursued by religious groups such as the Quakers and the Amish, and by secular groups such as pacifist socialists and others. Zweig was a pre-World War Two pacifist, as were many other European intellectuals, writers, artists and thinkers, many of them Jewish. During and after the war, however, Jewish reality in the world completely changed because of the systematic extermination of the Jewish people in Europe, known as the Holocaust. Jews once again, as happened in antiquity, became a warrior people, established a powerful Jewish army known as the Israel Defense Force, won several wars, and took their place again on the stage of history. While the State of Israel was established with the specific purpose of pursuing peace, it had to become a strong military power in order to survive. Here history repeated itself. When the Israelites under Moses arrived in the Promised Land, they had to become a warrior people to conquer Canaan. When they returned from the Babylonian exile under the leadership of Ezra and Nehemiah and sought to rebuild the Temple in Jerusalem, they faced resistance from other groups who had settled in the area and had to build the Temple "with one hand doing the work and the other holding a weapon" (Nehemiah 4:11). It will happen again during the destruction of the Second Temple around 70 CE, when the Jews had to face the mighty Roman legions, and after the destruction, in the time of the Bar Kokhba rebellion sixty years later. This rebellion, which lasted less than two years, resulted in the death of nearly half a million Jews, a staggering figure for the second century CE. It was so devastating, that for the next eighteen centuries Jews gave up the art of war and turned inwardly into what was in effect a pacifist existence.

A facile reading of the book of Jeremiah would lead one to conclude that while the Judeans were anxious to fight for their freedom, Jeremiah advocated submitting to the foreign occupiers. Worse yet, during the siege on Jerusalem in the time of King Zedekiah, Jeremiah advocates surrender, which was considered an act of treason.

To better understand Jeremiah's view of war and peace, let us consider the following: When King Josiah goes into battle against the Egyptian army that was traveling northward through his land on its way to Assyria, Jeremiah does not voice any opposition. When the young king dies on the battlefield, Jeremiah offers a lament for him. Similarly, when, a century earlier, Jerusalem comes under attack by the Assyrians, King Hezekiah asks the prophet Isaiah to intercede with the God of Israel, and Isaiah does with good results. When, however, it becomes clear to Jeremiah that fighting the Babylonians will only bring destruction and exile upon his people, he opts for survival rather than national suicide. The lesson here is clear: Hezekiah and Josiah were righteous kings. Their wars were just wars, therefore they could count on God's help. The other kings' wars were misguided and unrighteous, hence they could not count on God's help. Jewish tradition will later develop a theological view on obligatory or just war, or *milhemet mitzvah*, and voluntary or questionable war.[45] In our time, one could argue that the war such as the one launched by the Allies against the Axis nations was a just war, while a war such as the Vietnam War was a questionable war. Regardless of one's point of view, history does create a consensus on which wars have been justified and which have not. In some cases, however, this question never quite seems to reach a resolution.

3.

Poverty and Hunger

Poverty and hunger are world problems. Hunger is at the extreme end of poverty. The Hebrew prophets put a great emphasis on helping the poor. Amos put it very bluntly:

> For the three transgressions of Israel,
> Yeah, for the four, I will not reverse it:
> Because they sell the righteous for silver,
> And the poor for a pair of shoes. (Amos 2:6)

Clearly, after the Hebrews transitioned from a nomadic to an agricultural society following the conquest of Canaan, and even more so after they began to build thriving urban communities, class distinctions between rich and poor grew sharper. People became more callous and less caring, and in the streets of Samaria and Judah there were beggars and people asking for bread. The laws of Leviticus mandate that the hungry be fed. Thus, the corners of the field during harvest time must be left for the poor:

> And when you reap the harvest of your land
> you shall not wholly reap the corner of thy field,
> neither shall you gather the gleaning of your harvest;
> you shall leave them for the poor,
> and for the stranger: I am Adonai your God.
> (Leviticus 23:22)

Additionally, the priests were expected to give part of the Temple offerings to the poor. But these laws were not being carefully observed. As farmers and merchants grew richer, they became less charitable. This was in direct violation of the Mosaic law and the prophets lashed out against the offenders.

None o f this changed in the time of Jeremiah who continued in the tradition of his predecessors to decry the lack of regard for the poor. When Jeremiah chastises King Jehoiakim, who oppresses the poor, he remind him of his father, Josiah:

> He judged the cause of the poor and the needy,
> Then it was well. . . . (22:16)

What is interesting about both Judaism and Christianity, as well as Islam, is that all three religions seem to have institutionalized poverty. The concept of eradicating poverty does not appear in any of them. The poor, they appear to be saying, are a fact of life. They always existed, and they always will. Therefore, religion, which is expected to be charitable, must find ways to help the poor.

One of the great failures of the three monotheistic religions is the fact that they have not been able to establish a community or a society without poverty. It may be an inescapable fact of life that human beings can never be equally affluent, since some can better manage their affairs than others. But a society where some people starve, and where some cannot afford the bare necessities of life, is not a fully civilized society. The Hebrew prophets understood this premise, and made it the cornerstone of their prophetic message. The laws of the Torah, as we have seen, are very clear on this score.

When the biblical Hebrew concept of *tzedakah*, or giving to the poor, becomes the Christian concept of charity, a prophet like Jeremiah would not see it as a step forward, but rather as a step backward in the development of monotheism. The difference between the two lies in the origin of the two words. *Tzedakah* is derived from the Hebrew root tz-d-k, which means justice. Giving to the poor is not an option, but rather an obligation mandated by the Source of all Justice. Charity, on the other hand, is derived from the Latin word *caritas*, which means affection, or, if you will, Christian love. Love is voluntary, not obligatory. It is something wished for, not imperative, whereas justice is an imperative.

In our time, the thinking regarding poverty and hunger in the industrialized world has finally taken cognizance of the fact that a truly civilized world cannot accept these two ills as the inalterable state of the human race. Some years ago, U.S. President Lyndon Johnson declared a "War on Poverty." While this war is yet to be won, the concept has been established. In the twenty-first century, industrial countries are actively seeking solutions to world hunger and poverty, as well as disease and epidemics. While there is still a long way to go, at least a start has been made and one can only hope that future generations will do better in this regard than we have done in the past.

4.

Religious and Ideological Pluralism

The greatest danger to the future of humankind, besides the threat to the environment, is religious and ideological intolerance. Ideological intolerance in the twentieth century resulted in the death of hundreds of millions of people. In the new century, global Islamic terrorism is being fed by religious intolerance. But this form of intolerance is not limited to fanatic Islamists. It can be found among the other religions and ideologies of the world. It also operates on tribal and national levels. Bigotry and racism are still widespread in every corner of the planet, even among people who otherwise are law-abiding, kind and considerate. In my extensive travels in recent years I have encountered prejudice everywhere, and not necessarily among ignorant or callous people. These attitudes seem to be built into the human condition, and are extremely hard to eradicate. And yet the human race at this late date in history can no longer afford to entertain such attitudes. Unless and until we all realize that we are all fellow-travelers on a small and highly vulnerable planet, sharing a common fate, we are putting the future of all of us at risk. What all of this means is that religious or ideological exclusivism is suicidal. Our only hope as a species lies in pluralism.

One may argue: wasn't Jeremiah an exclusivist? Didn't he argue that his God was the only true God? In order to answer this question, one needs to explain what Jeremiah meant by an absolute God of the Universe, as opposed to other options.

Jeremiah was not concerned with abstract theology or the philosophy of religion. His concern was the welfare of his people and of the human race. One absolute God of the Universe meant the following: While human experience is pluralistic, namely, different people have different ways of looking at the world and of understanding their destinies, all are part of one human reality under one absolute principle governing the common origin of the human species, its common physical attributes, and its common destiny. People speak many different languages. They have different diets, different customs, different likes and dislikes. But, to borrow a phrase from the sages of the Talmud, no person's blood is redder than another person's,[46] Jew or Gentile, black or white, rich or poor. All are equal before the ultimate force in the universe. Thus, Jeremiah is fully aware of the differences between people, and never advocates in his visions of the future one human religion practiced by everyone. Like Isaiah before him, he sees "many nations coming together" to live in peace and harmony.

Isaiah explains this future state better than Jeremiah, when he describes the wolf living with the lamb (11:6). He is taking an example from nature, where the wolf is still a wolf, and the lamb is still a lamb. They have not changed their physical attributes, only they have changed their nature from victim and victimizer to a new breed of animal that can subsist without attacking and killing other species.

All of nature may not become domesticated in any foreseeable future. But human beings have the ability to tame their impulse for war and destruction. Let us hope it happens before it is too late.

5.

Ecology

In recent years I have traveled to some remote corners of the earth such as Alaska, the Amazon, the islands of the South Pacific, and more. I learned two things about our planet. It is a beautiful planet, rich in plant and animal life. I can still see the seemingly endless surge of salmon coming back to the Alaskan shore from its annual swim to Japan. I can see the catfish in the Amazon that sometimes reaches one hundred or more pounds. And I can see the stingray and the shark in the crystal-clear water of Bora Bora with whom I swam unharmed. At the same time, it is a small planet, where you can only go so far before you begin to retrace your steps. Many people on this planet have not had the good fortune of having such a global look at the world. To them, the world may seem endless. But there is nothing endless about our world. It has limited resources, the ground under our feet is fragile, and our ecosystem is extremely vulnerable. We are custodians of this planet. Someone has put us here—as the story of creation in Genesis explains it in simplistic way—to take care of it. And today, more so than ever before, its future is in our hands.

From the moment Jeremiah first hears the voice of God in the blossoming almond tree, he derives his inspiration from nature. Life begins in nature. We are born in nature and we die in nature. Without it, we are nothing. There was a time (and you can still see traces of it in places like Alaska, or the Amazon, or the South Sea islands) when the human race was young and Mother Nature took care of us. She let us pick a fruit off the tree, spear a fish out of the water, drink water from the brook, and it gave us fig leaves and other kinds of leaves to clothe ourselves, as some Polynesians still do. But for the majority of us, particularly in the industrialized world, those days are long gone. Mother Nature has grown older, and she now expects us to take care of her. There is an old Jewish saying: One mother can take care of ten children, but ten children can't take care of one mother. Like all sayings, it is only partially true. There are children who take care of their mother. It is time we all learn a lesson from such children.

Jeremiah and other Hebrew prophets were keenly aware of the symbiotic relation between man and nature. They did not worship nature as a deity or deities. They had discovered a force beyond nature, a force that negates the naturalistic observation that "might is right," and posits a higher law in nature, the law of "just is right." By doing so, they were the first to discover that man is not a slave of nature, a so-called "noble savage" who lives at the mercy of the natural gods, but rather a custodian of nature, someone who has been put on this earth to cultivate and protect nature. In Jeremiah's time, his people and other people were destroying nature by their immoral pagan practices. In our time, we are destroying nature because of our insatiable drive to take and exploit without giving back and preserving. The new paganism is greed, which today has become a global threat. Jeremiah said:

> I beheld the earth, and it was waste and void;
> And the heavens, and they had no light.
> I beheld the mountains, and, lo, they trembled,
> And all the hills moved back and forth.
> I beheld, and there was no man,
> And all the birds of the heavens had fled.   (4:23-25)

Jeremiah makes it clear to his contemporaries that this vision is a warning. It need not be this way. God has given humanity the power to destroy and to build, to uproot and to plant. The choice is clear.

6.

Organized Religion

The Hebrew prophets were iconoclasts. They were forever at odds with the custodians of organized religion, namely, the priests. They were critical of the sacrificial cult, which they often regarded as an escape from moral obligations. To them, organized religion for the most part was a failure. Jeremiah certainly stands in the forefront of this prophetic thinking. As we have seen earlier, he did not reject the temple cult, nor did he advocate its abolishment. In the spirit of the prophet Samuel who, in a sense, is the forerunner of the literary prophets, he put obedience to God's law of justice and morality ahead of cult and sacrifices. The answer to whether Jeremiah believed in organized religion is yes. He believed that people as a cohesive group or a social organism need structure. He did not question the social structure of his time, consisting of secular and religious leaderships. Both were necessary, as it was necessary for the people to have a leader who had the ultimate responsibility for their destiny. To Jeremiah, the social order was only viable if it operated under a unified belief in what he saw as the one and only Master of the Universe (Adonai means master). Clearly, a secular society to him would be a denial of that Supreme Being, without whom he would not have found meaning in the human endeavor. But then again, he was the last one to accept organized religion unquestioningly, warts and all. It was too important to him, and he would not accept it without questioning. Organized religion had to prove itself worthy of its mission.

One may wonder what Jeremiah would think about organized religion if he lived today and were aware of the history of monotheism during the past twenty centuries. Would he believe our world to be better off with or without organized religion?

Organized religion posits a belief in a Supreme Being. Surely, to Jeremiah this belief is a given. He would remind us that God gave humanity free will, whereby each person can choose between right and wrong. Organized religion is a human rather than a divine institution, hence it is bound to make wrong choices. Religious worship and ritual observance do not automatically grant purity of heart and the performance of good deeds. It is quite possible that Jeremiah would have expected organized religion by now to have done much more good in the world than it has. But it is doubtful that he would advocate doing away with it.

Organized religion over the centuries has been most successful on the individual and communal levels, not on the national or international or inter-group levels. It has brought great comfort and support to millions of individuals, either singly or in community. But it has not been successful, for the most part, in promoting peaceful coexistence among different groups of people and different belief systems. Here there is much to be done, and in the new century it is a matter of great urgency.

One could wonder what the world today would be like if there hadn't been a Jeremiah, or Hebrew prophets, or Christianity, or Islam. There is no way of knowing. We do know, however, that until recent times more than one half of the human race, namely, the people of Southeast and East Asia, has had little exposure to Western monotheism and pursued what is generally known as Eastern religions (more appropriately a combination of social philosophies and mythologies). Yet the East has been plagued by the same social and national ills as the West, and at no time in its history has managed to create a society based on equality, freedom and justice. All societies on this planet are yet to live up to the lofty teachings of their sages and prophets.

7.

Godliness

We have now taken a long journey with Jeremiah. We have looked at the great issues of his time and how he dealt with them, and we have also looked at the great issues of our time and how they appear through the prism of his utterances and his actions. We need to conclude our journey with the question: If we were to choose one word that would sum up Jeremiah's message, what would that word be?

I believe that word would be godliness. The usual definition of godliness is piety, living a life in keeping with God's word. But godliness can be defined much more broadly, and I believe Jeremiah would define it in the broadest way possible. Godliness does not necessarily mean being a church-goer or a mosque-goer or a synagogue-goer. It means, above all else, recognizing that every human being and every living thing is godly, deserving our respect. To live a life of godliness is to strive to be truthful, to be aware of the needs of others, and especially of their pain and suffering. It means to have a purpose in life other than self-gratification and self-indulgence. It means being always aware of life as a divine gift, and of the need to cultivate one's mind and soul and preserve one's health.

It means, in particular, being aware of the distinction between what one believes and what is *common human experience*, and to approach that distinction with humility. Thus, for example, if one believes in the afterlife, one has to allow for the fact that it is a belief, not an empirical fact. Hence, if someone else does not believe in an afterlife, that person should not be scorned, much less chastised. One can live a godly life without believing in an afterlife, or angels, or demons. And one can certainly live an ungodly life believing in all those things. The real test of godliness is humanness, namely, the way one treats others. The post-biblical Jewish sages explained that God prefers people to follow God's laws of righteousness rather than believe in God.[47] And the Christian Gospels tell us: "Whatsoever you do to the least of these, my brothers and sisters, you do unto me."

Jeremiah, while sitting in jail as Jerusalem is about to fall to the enemy, takes cognizance of the things that are beyond his human understanding—great prophet that he is—when God says to him:

> Thus said Adonai who is planning it,
> God who is shaping it to bring it about,
> Whose name is Adonai.

> Call Me, and I will answer you,
> And I will tell you wondrous things,
> Secrets you have not known. (33:2-3)

God does not tell Jeremiah about the afterlife, or about angels and demons. He does not offer him a vision of anything supernatural or eschatological. God simply tells Jeremiah what will happen after Jerusalem is destroyed:

> I will heal them and reveal to them
> Abundance of true favor. (33:6)

There, in this simple message, lies the entire truth. Our world needs healing. We need to heal our own souls, and we need to heal each other. When that day comes, the world will be redeemed.

Notes

1. "Archaeology has produced artifactual and inscriptional evidence touching on almost every aspect of the daily life of Judah in Jeremiah's time." Philip J. King, *Jeremiah: An Archaeological Companion* (Louisville, Kentucky: John Knox Press, 1989), xxi.

When does biblical history actually begin? This question is tied to the problem of the authorship of the Bible. If we are to follow the traditional Jewish belief, then Moses wrote the first five books of the Bible, which begin with the story of creation, and end with the death of Moses. The authorship of later books in the Bible is attributed to other major biblical figures. Thus, David is considered the author of most of the Psalms. His son, Solomon, is believed to be the author of the Song of Songs, Proverbs, and Ecclesiastes.

The first problem we face here is that while there is a good deal of physical evidence that allows us to reconstruct the ancient civilizations of the ancient Middle East, including many of its rulers and key figures, we are yet to find evidence of the existence of a Moses back in the 14th century BCE, or even a David and a Solomon three or four hundred years later. There are good reasons to believe that all of them did exist, as did the first ancestor of the Jews, Abraham, back in the 18th century BCE. But there is little doubt what we know about them was written down much later, mostly after their time, and therefore history and legend became commingled.

During the twentieth century, biblical archeology led by both Christian and Jewish scholars made some broad assumptions about the Hebrew Patriarchs, the stories of Moses, and the reign of Israel's two great kings—David and Solomon. Stables found in Megiddo were believed to be King Solomon's stables. Copper mines found near Elat were also attributed to that king. Records of an invasion of Egypt by Semitic tribes around the time of Moses were believed to be related to the Israelites, and so on. As the century aged and matured, many of these hypotheses were discarded. Many scholars now agree that the process of writing the Bible began after the time of Solomon, and reached a significant stage during the time of Jeremiah. At this time a much clearer separation of history and legend can be detected. This holds true in world history as well. Historiography as we know it today begins around that time in Greece, with historians like Herodotus and Thucydides who, unlike earlier writers, were not bound by royal or priestly coercion to exaggerate and embellish the historical records, but instead recorded the events of their time as they saw them. Jewish and Western civilizations in many ways begin around this time, when two numerically small nations—Greece and Israel—set the foundations of human reason, culture, and faith.

2. The prophetic imagery in the book of Jeremiah is dominated by the whole range of nature—land, sea and sky; hills, mountains and valleys; forests, rivers and desert; sun, moon and stars; wild and domestic animals; trees, plants and herbs; rain, storms and snow.

One of Jeremiah's favorite expressions is "birds of the sky and the beasts of the earth" (12:4; 15:3; 16:4; 31:13; 34:20), as an encompassing reference to the entire animal kingdom. He keeps referring to the desert as the place where spirit prevails over matter (2:2, 6, 31; 3:3), but also the place where people yearn for the "land of milk and honey" (11:5). In chapter 12 Jeremiah appears to be in a state of complete despair, because evildoers prosper, and because everyone has turned against him. In this state of extreme mental agitation his language becomes confused and his imagery is a tangle of nature metaphors, including the term *ayit tzavuah* (12:9) which is either a spotted bird of pray or a bird of prey and a hyena, both images of predatory animals. Other predatory animals are wolves (5:6), leopards (5:6; 13:23), and lions (2:30; 5:6; 12:9, 25:38; 50:17, 44; 51:38). The lion is used to invoke the wrath of God, and in one place Jeremiah refers to God as "roaring" (25:30). There are more than a few references to horses, either metaphorically, when he compares the rich young men of Jerusalem who try to seduce their friends' wives as "neighing horses," or as actual animals of war (4:13; 5.8, 6; 6:23; 8:6, 16; 12:5; 22:5; 31:39; 47:3; 50:37, 43). Elsewhere Jeremiah mentions migratory birds such as storks, turtledoves, swifts and cranes, all of them familiar with the seasons as they follow their migratory routes without fail, while the people of Israel fail to follow their God (8:7). Serepents and adders are mentioned as a form of punishment (8:17); the wild ass is a symbol of recklessness (2:24); the donkey's burial is a symbol of ignominious burial for the sinning king (22.19); the people are often compared to sheep and cattle (11:19; 34:18; 50:17). Also 3:25; 5:17; 31:11; 51:23). Other animals mentioned are doves (48:28), heifers (31:18), eagles (49:22), jackals (10:22; 14:6), deer (14:5), locust (51:14), and rams (34:18; 51:41). Examples of vegetation are vines (2:22; 5.17; 6:9; 8:13; 31:5; 48:32), figs (5:17; 8:13; 24:1-4; 29:18), palm (10:5), olive (11:16, 31.11), and cedar (22:15). Minerals include copper (6:28), iron (6:28; 11:4), silver and gold (10:4, 9). Another major source of nature images is water, ranging from cisterns (2:13) to brooks (2:13), to rivers (2:18), as well as various kinds of rain—showers, early rain, late rain (3:3; 5:28), rain storms (10:13), and also snow (18:14).

3. When he speaks his famous words, "I remember the kindness of your youth" (2:2), which rank among the Bible's most striking expressions of God's love for Israel.

4. Recent archeological discoveries include inscriptions in which Jews of the time of the First Temple refer to "Yahweh and his Asherah. See Kuntillet Ajrud inscription, 8th century BCE, discovered in 1975-6 by Israeli archeologist Ze'ev Meshel. See also William G. Dever, *Did God Have a Wife?* (Grand Rapids, Michigan: William B. Eerdmans, 2005).

5. There is a certain ambiguity as to the term "Queen of Heaven," since the unvocalized Hebrew word *mlkt* is indeed queen, but the vocalized word in this text becomes "the kingdom of." See Teresa Ann Ellis, "Jeremiah 44: What if 'the Queen of Heaven' is YHWH?" *Journal for the Study of the Old Testament* 33, no. 4 (2009).

6. See endnote 4 above.

7. It is interesting to note that the term "Hebrew" had taken on new meaning in the nineteenth and twentieth centuries, with the rebirth of Jewish nationalism. After eighteen centuries of Jewish existence without a Jewish sovereign state and without a spoken Hebrew language, Jewish nationalism or, more specifically, Zionism, reached back to the national origins of the Jewish people and its original language, and created a new dichotomy of Hebrew as the new Jew. Today in the State of Israel there are so-called secular Jews who still consider themselves Hebrews rather than Jews, although the general trend once again is to embrace the concept of Jew as a unifying concept for both Israeli and world Jewry.

8. See Richard E. Friedman, *Who Wrote the Bible?* (San Francisco, Harper San Francisco, 1989). Contemporary biblical scholarship continues to debate the theory of the Deuteronomistic school, according to which a whole school of writers wrote different parts of Deuteronomy and the historical books that follow it in the Hebrew Bible. Friedman argues for one author, and this writer is in agreement with his view.

9. An impression of the seal of Gemariah son of Shaphan was found in the City of David in Jerusalem in recent years.

10. There are references in those books to other historical records, especially of the period of the monarchy, such as the Annals of the Kings of Judah (II Kings 23:28), but none so far have been recovered.

11. See Israel Finkelstein and Amihai Mazar, *The Quest for the Historical Israel,* (Atlanta: Society of Biblical Literature, 2007).

12. This will remain the Jewish policy throughout the Diaspora for the next twenty-six centuries.

13. The words "to give you a future and a hope" are quoted on the wall at Yad Vashem, Israel's national Holocaust museum.

14. The name Pashhur was common among the priests of that period. An ostracon (inscribed potsherd) with this name was found in recent years.

15. We are reminded of the book of Job where the person after whom the book is named is being put through the worst trials a righteous man can be put through, and when his wife tells him to curse God so that he may die, he chooses instead to curse the day of his birth, quite the same way Jeremiah does:

Let the day perish wherein I was born,
And the night wherein it was said:
A man-child is brought forth.
Let that day be darkness;
Let not God inquire after it from above,
Neither let the light shine upon it.
Let darkness and the shadow of death
Claim it for their own;
Let a cloud dwell upon it; let all that
Maketh black the day terrify it.
As for that night, let thick darkness seize upon it;
Let it not rejoice among the days of the year;
Let it not come into the number of the months.
Lo, let that night be desolate;
Let no joyful voice come there. (Job 3:3-7)

16. See endnote 17 below.

17. Two of the most amazing archeological discoveries ever took place in Jerusalem in 2005 and 2008. In a site near the Old City identified as the royal palace of King David, which would have been the palace of King Zedekiah as well, the impressions of seals dating back to Jeremiah's time were found in the same place, the first bearing the name of Jucal the son of Shelemiah, and the second that of Gedaliah the son of Pashhur, two of the three court counselors mentioned in this story. Finding the personal belongings of a person mentioned in the Bible is extremely rare. Finding those of two persons mentioned in the same verse is unprecedented. Needless to say, these breathtaking discoveries give the story historical validity.

18. There must have been those in Jerusalem at that time who thought that if they could get rid of Jeremiah the fortune of war might change, since it was he rather than God causing their downfall.

19. Alternate name for Babylonians.

20. This passage is incorporated in the Passover Haggadah. It gained new tragic meaning after the Holocaust.

21. The traditional grave of Rachel is in Bethlehem, some 11 miles south of Ramah, yet the exact place of Rachel's burial place is not clear. It is somewhere between Ramah and Bethlehem. Here we have the symbolism of Jeremiah feeling Rachel's presence in the land of Benjamin, her beloved younger son, and near the land of Ephraim, the grandson of her older son, Joseph.

22. This event is marked by observing the Fast of Gedaliah.

23. "Archaeology has produced artifactual and inscriptional evidence touching on almost every aspect of the daily life of Judah in Jeremiah's time." (See endnote 1).

24. E.g., *shefaim, ayit tzavuah.*

25. Here Islam parts ways with the other two religions. Perhaps because Christianity regards one particular person as being the son of God, Islam went out of its way to reject the concept of the fatherhood of God.

26. Jeremiah accuses his people of saying to wood, "You are my father," and to stone, "You gave birth to me" (2:27).

27. The zeal of the Hebrew prophets will carry over to Christianity, whose missionaries over the centuries as they spread their faith around the world would not give non-Christian religions much quarter and would often physically destroy their places of worship, as I witnessed recently in Bora Bora, French Polynesia. Islam, for its part, has acted quite similarly.

28 See Exodus Raba, B'shalach, 21:6.

29. The second half of the book of Isaiah represents another, post-exilic prophet, now referred to as Deutero-Isaiah.

30. In the vision of the chariot he uses the obscure word *hashmal*, which later becomes the Hebrew word for electricity. (1:4)

31. See Mordecai Schreiber, "The Real Suffering Servant" Jerusalem; Jewish Bible Quarterly, Jan-Mar 2009.

32. The Hebrew original is extremely difficult to decipher, full of poetic terms that are barely intelligible. Extant English translations—both Jewish and non—are mostly guesswork. The following is my attempt at going a step beyond those translations in light of my understanding of Jeremiah.

33. R.E.O. White, *The Indomitable Prophet: A Biographical Commentary on Jeremiah.* Grand Rapids, Michigan: William Eerdmans, 1992, p. 13.

34. A linguistic analysis of Jeremiah-specific and Second Isaiah-specific Hebrew words and phrases reveals the following parallels:

Shoresh (root) – see Jer. 12:2, 17:8. Both Second Isaiah and Jeremiah talk about the rootedness of a person.

Eretz tziyah (arid land) – see Jer. 2:16. The arid land is where both the Israelites and the "suffering servant" come from.

Nivzeh (despised) – see Jer. 22:28. Refers to the low state of a person. In Second Isaiah it is the servant; in Jeremiah it is King Jehoiachin after he is exiled to Babylon.

Mastir panim (hides his face) – see Jer. 33:5; also 37:17, 38:16, 40:15. The theme of hiding and specifically of God hiding His face is common to both prophets.

Musar (lesson) – see Jer. 2:30, 5:3, 7:28, 17:23, 32:33, 35:13. This term is typical to Jeremiah.

Shlomeynu (our welfare) – see Jer. 29:7. Jeremiah tells the exiles in Babylon to pray for the welfare of Babylon, and by doing so, as the Second Isaiah points out, he ensured the welfare of his own people.

Ka'tzon ta'inu (we were lost like sheep) – see Jer. 50:6. Jeremiah often compares his people to sheep and cattle (11:19, 34:18, 50:17).

Seh la'tevach (lamb to the slaughter) – see Jer. 11:19. Refers to Jeremiah's passive attitude when confronting a possible execution.

35. White, op. cit., p. 14.

36. The story is full of contradictions. God tells Abraham to sacrifice his only son, when, in fact, Abraham had another son named Ishmael.

37. It is entirely possible that during the monarchic period the stature of David kept growing, and many legends were added to it—as continued to happen in later Jewish history—in disproportion to the real historical David. (See Finkelstein and Mazar, op. cit.)

38. The most concrete reference to afterlife or resurrection in the Hebrew Bible appears in the book of Daniel (12:2).

39. "Rabbi Jacob says: 'This world resembles a corridor leading to the next world. Prepare yourself in the corridor so that you may enter the main room'" (Mishna, Avot, Chapter 3, Mishna 21).

40. Midrash Tanchuma, Pikude.

41. "Treatise on Resurrection," New York: Ktav Publishing, 1982. In this treatise Maimonides limits physical resurrection as mentioned in the book of Daniel to a miracle or a sign from God wholly dependent on God's will which is beyond human comprehension. He makes it clear that in the "world to come" or the afterlife there is no physical resurrection, only a spiritual existence of the soul. He argues that it is not universal, and not related to the messianic age. It is clear that he goes out of his way to limit this belief as much as he can, which clearly buttresses the traditional Jewish emphasis on life here and now.

42. A famous jingle attributed to the English-French writer Hilaire Belloc runs:
How odd of God
To choose the Jews.
It was actually penned by a British wag named William Norman Ewer. It elicited a response from Cecil Browne:
"But not so odd
As those who choose
A Jewish God
But spurn the Jews.

43. See Isaiah 13:6, 9; Ezekiel 30:3; Joel 1:15; 2:1, 11: 3:4; Amos 5:18, 20; Obadiah 1:15; Malachi 3:23.

44. See Pope John Paul II, *On Jews and Judaism: 1979-1987*, Eugene J. Fisher, Leon Klenicki, U.S. Catholic Conference 1987.

45. Maimonides, *Mishneh Torah, Sefer shoftim, hilchot melakhim* 5:1, Jerusalem: Mosad harav Kook, 1960.

46. *Pesachim* 25b.

47. *Pesiqta de-Rav Kahana* 15,5. New York: JTS Press, 1963.

Bibliography

Blank, Sheldon, *Jeremiah: Man and Prophet*. Cincinnati, Hebrew Union College Press, 1961.

Bright, John, *Jeremiah* (The Anchor Bible). New York: Doubleday, 1965.

Brueggemann, Walter, *The Theology of the Book of Jeremiah*. New York: Cambridge University Press, 2007.

———. *Like Fire in the Bones: Listening for the Prophetic Word in Jeremiah*. Minneapolis: Fortress Press, 2006.

———. *A Commentary on Jeremiah: Exile and Homecoming*. Grand Rapids, MI: William B. Eerdmans Publishing Company, 1998.

Carroll, Robert, *Jeremiah: A Commentary*. Philadelphia: Westminster, 1986.

Coogan, D. Michael, *A Brief Introduction to the Old Testament*. New York: Oxford University Press, 2009.

Dever, William G., *Did God Have a Wife?* Grand Rapids, MI: William B. Eerdmans Publishing Company, 2005.

Ellis, Teresa Ann, "Jeremiah 44: What if 'the Queen of Heaven' is YHWH?" *Journal for the Study of the Old Testament* 33, no. 4 (2009), 465-488.

Finkelstein, Israel, and Amihai Mazar, *The Quest for the Historical Israel*. Atlanta: Society of Biblical Literature, 2007.

Freedman, Rabbi Dr. H., Commentary by, *Jeremiah*. London: The Soncino Press Ltd., 1959.

Friedman, Richard E., *Who Wrote the Bible*. San Francisco: Harper San Francisco, 1989.

Heschel, Abraham J., *The Prophets*. Philadelphia: The Jewish Publication Society of America, 1962.

Hoffman, Yair, *Jeremiah, Introduction and Commentary* (in Hebrew). Tel Aviv: Am Oved, 2001.

Holladay, William L., *Jeremiah 1: A Commentary on the Book of the Prophet Jeremiah, Chapters 1-25*. Philadelphia: Fortress, 1986.

Kaufmann, Yehezkel. *The Religion of Israel*. Chicago: University of Chicago Press, 1960.

King, Philip J., *Jeremiah: An Archaeological Companion*. Louisville, KY: Westminster/John Knox Press, 1993.

Kohn, Risa Levitt, and William H. C. Propp, "The Name of 'Second Isaiah': The Forgotten Theory of Nehemiah Rabban." Pp. 223-235 in *Fortunate the Eyes that See: Essays in Honor of David Noel Freedman*, edited by Astrid B. Beck, Andrew H. Bartlet, Paul R. Raabe and Chris A. Franke. Grand Rapids, MI: William B. Eerdmans Publishing Company, 1995.

Nicholson E. W., Commentary by, *The Book of the Prophet Jeremiah*, 1-25. New York:

Cambridge University Press, 1973.

———. *The Book of the Prophet Jeremiah*, 26-52. New York: Cambridge University Press, 1975.

Pietersma, Albert, and Benjamin G. Wright, eds., *A New English Translation of the Septuagint*. New York: Oxford University Press, 2007.

Rubenstein, Richard E., *Thus Saith the Lord: The Revolutionary Moral Vision of Isaiah and Jeremiah*. Orlando, FL: Harcourt, 2006.

Schreiber, Mordecai, "Jeremiah as the First Teacher of the Torah." *CCAR Journal* 217, no. 3 (Summer 2008): 11-21.

———. "The Real 'Suffering Servant': Decoding a Controversial Passage in the Bible." *The Jewish Bible Quarterly* 145, no. 1 (January-March 2009): 35-44.

Welch, A. C., Jeremiah: *His Time and His Work*. Oxford: Basil Blackwell, 1955.

White, R. E. O., The Indomitable Prophet: *A Biographical Commentary on Jeremiah*. Grand Rapids, MI: William B. Eerdmans Publishing Company, 1992.

Wright, J. Edwards, *Baruch ben Neriah*. Columbia, SC: University of South Carolina Press,
2003.

Index of Biblical Passages

Index

About the Author

Mordecai Schreiber is the author of fifty-two books on linguistic and Judaic topics. He has translated several books from Hebrew into English, and has published scholarly articles in both languages. He is the editor of *The Shengold Jewish Encyclopedia*, and the author of *Light to the Nations* and *Ask the Bible* (under the pen name Morry Sofer). He has taught Bible courses at Hoftra University and has lectured widely on biblical topics in the U.S., Israel and Central America.

The author was born and raised in Israel, and received his graduate degree and rabbinical ordination at the Hebrew Union College-Jewish Institute of Religion in New York in 1965, where he studied under world-renowned biblical scholars such as Nelson Glueck and Harry M. Orlinsky. He has been active for many years in interfaith activities, and has been an avid student of both the Hebrew Bible and the New Testament. He recently retired as publisher of Jewish and language books, and has since dedicated himself exclsuively to writing and lecturing.